The Gallic Wars

The Gallic Wars

By

Julius Caesar

The Gallic Wars by Julius Caesar. Translated by Thomas Holmes. First published in 1908. Revised translation © 2017 Enhanced Media Publishing.

First Printing: 2017.

ISBN: 9781549920004.

Contents

BOOK I

Campaigns against the Helvetii and Ariovistus

Gaul, taken as a whole, is divided into three parts, one of which is inhabited by the Belgae, another by the Aquitani, and the third by a people who call themselves Celts and whom we call Gauls. These peoples differ from one another in language, institutions, and laws. The Gauls are separated from the Aquitani by the river Garonne, from the Belgae by the Marne and the Seine. Of all these peoples the bravest are the Belgae; for they are furthest removed from the civilization and refinement of the Province, traders very rarely visit them with the wares which tend to produce moral enervation, and they are nearest to the Germans, who dwell on the further side of the Rhine, and are constantly at war with them. For the same reason the Helvetii also are braver than the other Gauls; they are fighting almost daily with the Germans, either trying to keep them out of their own country or making raids into theirs. That part of the whole country which, as we have said, is occupied by the Gauls, begins at the river Rhone, and is bounded by the Garonne, the Ocean, and the country of the Belgae. It extends, moreover, in the region occupied by the Sequani and the Helvetii, to the Rhine; and its trend is towards the north. The territory of the Belgae, commencing from the most distant frontier of Gaul, extends to the lower Rhine, and has a northerly and easterly aspect. Aquitania extends from the Garonne to the Pyrenees and that part of the Ocean which is off the coast of Spain; and its outlook is towards the north-west.

Pre-eminent among the Helvetii in rank and wealth was Orgetorix. In the consulship of Marcus Messala and Marcus Piso he organized a conspiracy among the nobles in the hope of making himself king, and persuaded the community to undertake a national emigration, as, being the most warlike of all the Gallic peoples, they could easily achieve dominion over the whole of Gaul. He had no difficulty in convincing them, because their country is limited everywhere by natural features, on one side by the Rhine, a broad deep river, which separates the Helvetian territory from the Germans; on another by the lofty range of the Jura, between the Helvetii and the Sequani; on a third by the Lake of Geneva and the Rhone, which separates our Province from the Helvetii. These Hermits restricted their movements and made it comparatively difficult for them to attack their neighbors; and, being a warlike people, they chafed under this restraint. Moreover, considering their numbers and their renown as valiant warriors, they felt that their territories —only two hundred and forty miles long by one hundred and eighty broad—were too small.

Impelled by these motives and swayed by Orgetorix, they determined to emigrate into Gaul: buying up all the draught cattle and wagons that they could obtain, bringing all available lands under cultivation, with the object of securing an abundance of grain for the journey, and establishing relations of peace and amity with the neighboring tribes. They believed that two years would be sufficient to complete these preparations, and passed an enactment fixing their departure for the third year. Orgetorix was chosen as leader, and undertook a mission to the several tribes. In the course of his tour he persuaded a Sequanian named Casticus, whose father, Catamantaloedes, had for many years held sovereignty over the Sequani, and had been honored by the Roman Senate with the title of Friend, to seize the royal power, which his father had held before him, over his own tribe; he also persuaded Dumnorix, an Aeduan, brother of Diviciacus, who at that time held the principal power in his own country, and was very popular with the masses, to make a similar attempt, and gave him his daughter in marriage. He convinced them that it would be quite easy to achieve their purpose, as he was going to seize sovereignty over his own tribe; the Helvetii were undoubtedly the strongest people in the whole of Gaul; and he affirmed that by his wealth and his armed force he would secure them the possession of their thrones. Enthralled by his eloquence, they swore mutual fidelity; and they hoped that, once they had secured their thrones, they would be able, backed by three powerful and stable peoples, to make themselves masters of the whole of Gaul.

The scheme was made known to the Helvetii by informers. In accordance with national Helvetian custom, they insisted that Orgetorix should plead suicide. If he were condemned, his inevitable punishment would be death at the stake. On the day fixed for the pleading he made all his slaves from all parts, numbering ten thousand, come to the trial, and marched thither at the head of all his retainers and debtors, who were very numerous. With their protection he escaped trial. Exasperated at this defiance, the community endeavored to assert their rights by force, and the authorities summoned a posse from the districts, when Orgetorix died; and there is some reason to suspect (so the Helvetii believe) that he died by his own hand.

After his death the Helvetii in no way relaxed their efforts to carry out their intended emigration. As soon as they believed themselves ready for the enterprise, they set fire to all their strongholds, of which there were twelve, their villages, numbering four hundred, and the remaining buildings, which belonged to individuals; and burned the whole of their grain, except what they were going to take with them, that they might have no hope of returning home, and so be more ready to face every danger. Every man was directed to take a supply of flour from his house for three months for his own use. They induced their neighbors, the Rauraci, the Tulingi and the Latobrigi, to join their enterprise, burn their strongholds and villages, and emigrate along with them; at the same time they formed a close alliance with the Boii, who had formerly dwelt on the further bank of the Rhine, and had migrated into Noricum and taken Noreia.

There were only two routes by which it was possible for them to leave their country. One, a march leading through the country of the Sequani, passing between the Jura and the Rhone, was so narrow and difficult that carts could barely pass along it one at a time, while a lofty mountain overhung it, so that a handful of men could easily stop them; the other, leading through our Province, is much easier and more convenient, for the Rhone, which flows between the country of the Helvetii and that of the Allobroges, who had recently been subdued, is, at certain points, fordable. Geneva, the most remote town belonging to the Allobroges, is connected by a bridge with the country of the Helvetii, to which it is quite close. The Helvetii believed that they could either induce the Allobroges to let them pass through their country, as they were not yet apparently well disposed towards the Romans, or could compel them to do so. When everything was ready for their departure, they fixed the March 28 in the consulship of Lucius Piso and Aulus Gabinius, for the general muster on the banks of the Rhone.

As soon as Caesar was informed that they were attempting to march through the Province, he promptly quit the capital, pushed on as fast as he could possibly travel into Further Gaul, and made his way to the neighborhood of Geneva. As the entire force in Further Gaul amounted only to one legion, he ordered as many troops as possible to be raised throughout the Province, and directed that the bridge at Geneva should be broken down. The Helvetii, on being informed of his approach, sent an embassy to him, composed of their most illustrious citizens, headed by Nammeius and Verucloetius, to say that they purposed, with his consent, to march through the Province, as there was no other route open to them, but that they would do no harm. Caesar, remembering that Lucius Cassius, when consul, had been slain by the Helvetii, and his army defeated and forced to pass under the yoke, was not disposed to grant their request; and he was of opinion that men of hostile temper were not likely to refrain from outrage and mischief. Still, in order to gain time for his levies to assemble, he told the envoys that he would take some days for consideration: if they had any favor to ask, they might return on April 13.

Meantime, employing the legion which he had with him and the troops which had assembled from the Province, he constructed a rampart sixteen feet high and a trench from the Lake of Helvetii to Geneva, which overflows into the Rhone, to the passage Jura, which separates the territory of the Sequani from the Helvetii—a distance of nineteen miles. When these works were finished he constructed redoubts to enable him to repel the Helvetii, in case they attempted to force a passage. When the appointed day came round, and the envoys returned, he told them that he could not, consistently with the established usage of the Roman People, allow anyone to march through the Province; and he warned them that, if they attempted to use force, he would stop them. The disappointed Helvetii lashed barges together and made a number of rafts, while others forded the Rhone at the shallowest parts, sometimes in the day, but oftener at night, and tried to break through; but, foiled by the entrenchments, the rapid concentration of the troops, and their volleys of missiles, they abandoned their attempt.

There remained only the route through to the Sequani; and it was so narrow that they could not advance if the Sequani objected. Being unable to win their consent by their own efforts, they sent envoys to the Aeduan, Dumnorix, hoping, by his intercession, to gain their object. Dumnorix had great influence with the Sequani from his personal popularity and lavish bribery, and was well disposed towards the Helvetii, having married a daughter of Orgetorix, who belonged to that tribe: moreover, his desire of royal power made him eager for revolution, and he wished to lay as many tribes as possible under obligations to himself. Accordingly he undertook the mission. He induced the Sequani to allow the Helvetii to pass through their territory, and affected an exchange of hostages between the two peoples, the Sequani undertaking not to obstruct the march of the Helvetii, the Helvetii to abstain from mischief and outrage.

Caesar was informed that the Helvetii intended to march through the country of the Sequani and the Aedui into the territories of the Santones, which are not far distant from those boundaries of the Tolosates, which is a state in the Province. If this took place, he saw that it would be attended with great danger to the Province to have warlike men, enemies of the Roman people, bordering upon an open and very fertile tract of country. For these reasons he placed Titus Labienus, one of his generals, in charge of the entrenchments which he had constructed; hastened to Italy by forced marches; raised two legions there; withdrew three from their winter quarters in the neighborhood of Aquileia; and advanced rapidly with all five by the shortest road leading over the Alps into Further Gaul. The Ceutrones, Graioceli, and Caturiges seized the Alpine heights and tried to stop the advance of the army. Beating them off in several combats, he made his way in seven days from Ocelum, the extreme point of the Cisalpine Province, into the territory of the Vocontii in the Further Province: thence he led the army into the country of the Allobroges, and from their country into that of the Segusiani, the first people outside the Province, beyond the Rhone.

The Helvetii had by this time threaded their forces over through the narrow defile and the territories of the Sequani, and had arrived at the territories of the Aedui, and were ravaging their lands. The Aedui, unable to defend themselves or their property against their attacks, sent a deputation to Caesar to ask for help, pleading that they had at all times deserved well of the Roman People, and it was not right that their lands should be ravaged, their children carried off into slavery, and their towns captured almost under the eyes of our army. At the same time the Ambarri, who were connected with the Aedui by friendship and blood, informed Caesar that their lands had been laid waste, and that it was more than they could do to repel the enemy's attacks upon their towns. The Allobroges also, who possessed villages and estates on the further side of the Rhone, fled to Caesar, alleging that they had nothing left except the bare soil. For these reasons Caesar decided that it would be unwise to wait till his allies had lost all that they possessed, and the Helvetii reached the country of the Santoni.

A river called the Saone flows through the territories of the Aedui and Sequani into the Rhone with such incredible slowness, that it cannot be determined by the eye in which direction it flows. This the Helvetii were crossing by rafts and boats joined together. Learning from his patrols that about one-fourth were still on the near side of the river, while three-fourths had passed over, Caesar started from his camp in the third watch, with three legions, and came up with the division which had not yet crossed. Attacking them unexpectedly while their movements were impeded, he destroyed a great many: the rest took to flight and concealed themselves in the neighboring woods. The clan in question was called the Tigurini, the entire Helvetian community being divided into four clans. This clan, acting independently, had emigrated within the memory of our fathers, and made the army of the consul, Lucius Cassius, who was himself killed, pass under the yoke. Thus, either by accident or divine providence, that section of the Helvetian community which had brought a signal disaster upon the Roman People was the first to pay the penalty. In this action Caesar avenged a family wrong as well as the wrongs of his country; for a general named Lucius Piso, the grandfather of his father-in-law, Lucius Piso, had perished in the same battle as Cassius at the hands of the Tigurini.

After fighting this action, Caesar bridged the Saone with the object of pursuing the rest of the Helvetian force, and thereby conveyed his army across. The Helvetii, seeing that he had effected in a single day the passage of the river, which they had accomplished with the greatest difficulty in twenty days, and alarmed by his unexpected advance, sent an embassy to meet him, headed by Divico, who had commanded in the campaign against Cassius. He addressed Caesar in the following terms:—if the Roman People would make peace with the Helvetii, they would go wherever Caesar fixed their abode, and would remain there; but if he persisted in his hostile attitude, he would do well to remember the disaster which had befallen the Roman People in the past and the ancient valour of the Helvetii. Granted that he had surprised one clan at a moment when their countrymen had crossed the river and could not help them, he need not therefore exaggerate his own prowess, or look down upon them. The lesson they had learned from their fathers and their forefathers was to fight like men, and not to rely upon trickery or ambuscade. Let him not, then, suffer the place where they stood to derive its name from a Roman reverse and from the annihilation of an army, or bequeath the remembrance thereof to posterity.

Caesar replied that he had no reason to hesitate, because he well-remembered the events which the Helvetian envoys had recounted; and he remembered them with indignation, for the Roman People had not deserved what had befallen them. If they had been conscious of wrong-doing it would have been easy to take precautions; but they had been deceived because they were not conscious of having done anything to justify alarm, and saw no necessity for taking alarm without reason. Even if he were willing to forget an old affront, how could he banish the recollection of fresh outrages,—their attempt to force a passage through the Province in despite of him, and their raids upon the Aedui, the Ambarri, and the Allobroges? The insolence with which they boasted of their victory, their astonishment at his having so long put up with their outrages, pointed to the same conclusion. For it was the wont of the immortal gods sometimes to grant prosperity and long impunity to men whose crimes they were minded to punish in order that a complete reverse of fortune might make them suffer more bitterly. Still, notwithstanding this, if they would give hostages to satisfy him that they intended to fulfil their promises, and if they would recompense the Aedui for the wrongs which they had done to them and likewise the Allobroges, he would make peace with them. Divico replied that, as the Roman People could testify, the Helvetii, following the maxims of their ancestors, were in the habit of receiving hostages, not of giving them. With this rejoinder he withdrew.

Next day the Helvetii quitted their march up the valley encampment. Caesar did the same, and sent on ahead all his cavalry, amounting to four thousand, which he had raised from the whole Province, from the Aedui, and from their allies, to see in what direction the enemy was going. Following the rearguard too eagerly, they engaged the Helvetian cavalry on unfavorable ground, and a few of our men fell. Elated at having repulsed such a numerous body of cavalry with five hundred horsemen, the Helvetii more than once halted boldly, their rearguard challenging our men. Caesar would not allow his men to fight, and for the time he thought it enough to prevent the enemy from looting, foraging, and ravaging the country. The two armies marched in close company for about a fortnight, the enemy's rear and our van never being more than five or six miles apart.

Meanwhile Caesar daily called upon the Aedui for the grain which, as he reminded them, they had promised in the name of their Government. Gaul being situated, as the narrative has shown, beneath a northern sky, the climate is cold, and therefore not only was the standing corn unripe, but there was not even a sufficient supply of fodder; while Caesar was unable to use the grain which he had brought up the Saone in barges, because the Helvetii had struck off from that river, and he was unwilling to move away from them. From day to day the Aedui kept him on the expectant, affirming that the grain was being collected—was on the way—was just at hand. When the day on which the men's rations would be due was near, feeling that his patience had been tried too long, he assembled their leading men, of whom he had a large number in camp; amongst others Diviciacus and Liscus, the chief magistrate — the Vergobret, as the Aedui call him—who is elected annually, and possesses the power of life and death over his countrymen. Caesar took them seriously to task for not helping him in this critical conjuncture, when the enemy were near and it was impossible either to buy corn or to get it from the fields, especially as he had undertaken the campaign in compliance with the entreaties of many of their own representatives. But what he complained of more seriously still was that they had played him false.

Then at length Liscus, moved by Caesar's speech, disclosed what he had hitherto kept secret. There were certain individuals, he said, who had great influence with the masses, and unofficially had more power than the magistrates themselves. These men made seditious and violent speeches, and worked upon the fears of the people to prevent them from contributing their due quota of grain. It would be better, they argued, supposing that the Aedui could not for the moment win supremacy over Gaul, to have Gauls for their masters than Romans; and they had no doubt that, if the Romans overpowered the Helvetii, they would deprive the Aedui of their liberty, along with the rest of Gaul. These men kept the enemy informed of our plans, and of all that was going on in camp, and they were beyond his control. What was more, he knew that, in making these revelations to Caesar, which he had only done under pressure, he had acted at great personal risk, and for that reason he had kept silent as long as he could.

Caesar perceived that Liscus's remarks pointed to Dumnorix, the brother of Diviciacus; but, as he did not want these matters to be talked about with a number of people present, he promptly dismissed the assembly, only detaining Liscus. When they were alone, he questioned him about what he had said in the meeting. Liscus spoke unreservedly and boldly. Caesar put the same questions to others separately, and found that what Liscus said was true. The individual referred to was Dumnorix, a man of boundless audacity, extremely popular with the masses from his open-handedness, and an ardent revolutionary. For many years he had farmed at a low rate and monopolized the Aeduan tolls and all the other taxes, as, when he made a bid, no one dared to bid against him. In this way he had increased his fortune and amassed large sums to expend in bribery; he permanently maintained at his own expense a large body of horsemen, whom he kept in attendance upon him; he possessed great influence not only in his own country, but also with the surrounding tribes; and, to strengthen this influence, he had arranged a marriage for his mother with a Biturigian of the highest rank and the greatest authority, while his own wife was a Helvetian, and he had arranged marriages for his sister on the mother's side and his female relations among other tribes. From his connection with the Helvetii, he was a partisan of theirs and well disposed towards them and he also personally detested Caesar and the Romans, because their coming had lessened his power and restored his brother, Diviciacus, to his former influential and honorable position. If anything should befall the Romans, he saw great reason to hope that, by the aid of the Helvetii, he would secure the throne; while, so long as the Roman People were supreme, he despaired not only of making himself king, but even of retaining his existing influence. Caesar also found, in the course of his inquiries, that, in the disastrous cavalry combat a few days before, it was Dumnorix with his troopers (for he commanded the auxiliary cavalry which the Aedui had sent to Caesar) who had set the example of flight, and that, on their flight, the rest of the cavalry had taken alarm.

After learning these circumstances, since to these suspicions the most unequivocal facts were added, viz., that he had led the Helvetii through the territories of the Sequani; that he had provided that hostages should be mutually given; that he had done all these things, not only without any orders of his [Caesar's] and of his own state's, but even without their [the Aedui] knowing anything of it themselves; that he [Dumnorix] was reprimanded by the [chief] magistrate of the Aedui; he [Caesar] considered that there was sufficient reason why he should either punish him himself, or order the state to do so. There was one objection. Caesar had come to know that Diviciacus, Dumnorix's brother, felt the utmost devotion to the Roman People and the utmost goodwill towards himself, and that his loyalty, equity, and good sense were quite exceptional; in fact, he was afraid of offending Diviciacus by punishing his brother. Accordingly, before taking any definite step, he sent for Diviciacus, and, dismissing the ordinary interpreters, conversed with him through the medium of Gaius Valerius Troucillus, a leading Provincial and an intimate friend of his own, whom he trusted absolutely in all matters. Reminding Diviciacus of what had been said about Dumnorix at the meeting, when he was present, and at the same time telling him what everyone had separately said about him when alone with himself, he urgently requested him to consent to his either personally trying Dumnorix and passing judgement upon him, or else calling upon the state to do so, and not to take offence.

Bursting into tears, Diviciacus embraced but accepted Caesar and entreated him not to take severe measures against his brother. Caesar knew, he said, that the story was true, and no one suffered more under his brother's conduct than himself; for at a time when his own influence was paramount with his countrymen and in the rest of Gaul, and his brother, on account of his youth, was powerless, the latter had risen through his support; and the resources and strength which he thus acquired he used not only to weaken his influence, but almost to ruin him. Public opinion as well as fraternal affection had weight with him. If Dumnorix were severely dealt with by Caesar, then, considering his own friendly relations with the latter, no one would believe that he was not responsible; and the result would be that the feeling of the whole country would turn against him. He continued pleading at great length and with tears when Caesar grasped his hand, reassured him, and begged him to say no more, telling him that he valued his friendship so highly that, out of regard for his loyalty and his intercession, he would overlook both political injury and personal grievance. He then called Dumnorix, keeping his brother, by; pointed out what he had to find fault with in his conduct; stated what he knew about him, and the complaints which his own countrymen brought against him; warned him to avoid giving any ground for suspicion in the future; and told him that he would overlook the past for his brother Diviciacus's sake. Nevertheless he placed Dumnorix under surveillance, in order to ascertain what he was doing and who were his associates.

On the same day Caesar was informed by his patrols that the enemy had encamped at the foot of a hill eight miles from his own camp, and accordingly sent a party to reconnoiter the hill and find out what the ascent was like from the rear. They reported that it was quite practicable. In the third watch he explained his plans to Titus Labienus, his second-in-command, and ordered him to ascend to the summit of the hill with two legions, taking the party who had ascertained the route as guides. In the fourth watch he marched in person against the enemy, following the route by which they had advanced and sending on all the cavalry in front. Publius Considius, who was considered a thorough soldier, and had served in the army of Lucius Sulla and afterwards in that of Marcus Crassus, was sent on in advance with patrols.

At daybreak Labienus was in possession of the summit of the hill, while Caesar was not more than a mile and a half from the enemy's camp, and, as he afterwards learned from prisoners, his own approach and that of Labienus were alike unknown, when Considius rode up to him at full gallop, and stated that the hill which he had desired Labienus to occupy was in possession of the enemy, as he could tell from the arms and crests being Gallic. Caesar withdrew his troops to a hill close by, and formed them in line of battle. Labienus, acting on Caesar's order not to engage until he saw his force close to the enemy's camp, so that they might be attacked on all sides at once, kept possession of the hill, waiting for the appearance of our men, and declined an engagement. At length, late in the day, Caesar learned from his patrols that the hill was in the possession of his own troops, that the Helvetii had moved off, and that Considius from panic had reported as a fact actually seen what he had not seen at all. The same day Caesar followed the enemy at the usual interval, and pitched his camp three miles from theirs.

Next day, as the rations of the army would be due in just forty-eight hours, and Caesar was not more than eighteen miles from Bibracte —by far the wealthiest and most important town of the Aedui—he thought it time to secure his supplies, and accordingly struck off from the route followed by the Helvetii and marched rapidly for Bibracte. The move was reported to the enemy by deserters from Lucius Aemilius, who commanded a troop of Gallic cavalry. The Helvetii, believing that the Romans were moving away because they were afraid of them (especially as on the day before, though they had occupied a position of vantage, they had declined an action), or confident of being able to cut them off from supplies, altered their plans, reversed their march, and began to hang upon our rearguard and harass them.

Observing this, Caesar withdrew his troops on to a hill close by and sent his cavalry to stem the enemy's attack. Meanwhile he formed his four veteran legions in three lines half-way up the hill, posting the two which he had recently levied in Cisalpine Gaul and all the auxiliaries above on the ridge, and thus occupying the whole hill; at the same time he ordered the men's packs to be collected and the space which they covered to be entrenched by the troops posted on the high ground. The Helvetii, following with all their wagons, parked their baggage, repulsed our cavalry with their dense array, and, forming a phalanx, moved up against our first line.

Caesar sent first his own charger and then the chargers of all the officers out of sight, in order, by putting all on an equality, to banish the idea of flight; then he harangued his men, and the battle began. The legionaries, throwing their javelins from their commanding position, easily broke the enemy phalanx, and, having destroyed their formation, drew their swords and charged. The Gauls were greatly hampered in action by the fact that in many cases several shields were transfixed and pinned together by the impact of one javelin, and, as the iron bent, they could not pull the javelins out or fight properly with their left arms encumbered, so that many, after repeated jerks, preferred to drop their shields and fight bare. At length, enfeebled by wounds, they began to fall back and retreat towards a hill about a mile off. They had gained the hill and the Romans were following after them, when the Boii and Tulingi, some fifteen thousand strong, who closed the enemy's column and served as the rearguard, marched up, immediately attacked the Romans on their exposed flank, and lapped round them; observing this, the Helvetii who had retreated to the hill began to press forward again and renewed the battle. The Romans effected a change of front and advanced in two divisions, the first and second lines to oppose the enemy when they had beaten and driven off; the third to withstand the newcomers.

Thus two battles went on at once, and the fighting was prolonged and fierce. When the enemy could no longer withstand the onslaughts of the Romans, one division drew back, up the hill, while the other withdrew to their baggage and wagons,—withdrew, not fled, for throughout the whole of this battle, though the fighting lasted from the seventh hour till evening, none could see an enemy in flight. Till far into the night fighting actually went on by the baggage; for the enemy had made a rampart of their wagons, and from their commanding position hurled missiles against our men as they came up, while some got between the wagons and behind the wheels and threw darts and javelins, which wounded our men. After a long struggle our men took possession of the baggage. Orgetorix's daughter and one of his sons were captured on the spot. About one hundred and thirty thousand souls survived the battle and fled without halting throughout the whole of that night. Three days later they reached the country of the Lingones, for our troops remained on the field for three days, out of consideration for their wounded and to bury the dead, and therefore were unable to pursue. Caesar sent dispatches and messages to the Lingones, warning them not to supply the fugitives with corn or otherwise assist them, and threatening that, if they did so, he would treat them as he had treated the Helvetii. After an interval of three days he started with his whole force in pursuit.

The Helvetii, under stress of utter destitution, sent envoys to Caesar to propose surrender. The envoys met him on the march, prostrated themselves before him, and in suppliant terms besought him with tears for peace. He told them that the fugitives must remain where they were and await his arrival; and they promised obedience. When Caesar reached the spot, he re-required the Helvetii to give hostages and to surrender their arms and the slaves who had deserted to them. While the hostages and deserters were being searched for and the arms collected, night came on, and about six thousand men, belonging to the clan known as the Verbigeni, quitted the Helvetian encampment in the early part of the night and pushed on for the Rhine and the territory of the Germans. Either they were afraid that after surrendering their arms they would be punished, or they hoped to get off scot-free, believing that, as the number which had surrendered was so vast, their flight might escape detection or even remain entirely unnoticed. When Caesar discovered this, he ordered the peoples through whose territories they had gone to hunt them down and bring them back if they wished him to hold them guiltless. When they were brought back he treated them as Aedui enemies; but all the rest, after they had delivered up hostages, arms, and deserters, he admitted to surrender. He ordered the Helvetii, Tulingi, and Latobrigi to return to their own country, whence they had come; and, as all their corn and pulse were gone, and they had not in their own country the means of satisfying their hunger, he directed the Allobroges to supply them with corn, and ordered them to rebuild the towns and villages which they had burned. His chief reason for doing this was that he did not wish the region which the Helvetii had abandoned to remain uninhabited, lest the Germans, who dwelt on the further side of the Rhine, might be induced by the fertility of the land to migrate from their own country into theirs, and establish themselves in proximity to the Province of Gaul, and especially to the Allobroges. The Aedui begged to be allowed to find room for the Boii within their own country, as they were a people of eminent and proved courage; and Caesar granted their request. The Aedui assigned them lands, and afterwards admitted them to the enjoyment of rights and liberties on equality with their own.

Documents, written in Greek characters, were found in the encampment of the Helvetii and brought to Caesar. They contained a schedule, giving the names of individuals, the, number of emigrants capable of bearing arms, and likewise, under separate heads, the numbers of old men, women, and children. The aggregate amounted to two hundred and sixty-three thousand Helvetii, thirty-six thousand Tulingi, thirteen thousand Latobrigi, twenty-three thousand Rauraci, and thirty-two thousand Boii. The number capable of bearing arms was ninety-two thousand, and the grand total three hundred and sixty-eight thousand. A census was taken, by Caesar's orders, of those who returned home; and the number was found to be one hundred and ten thousand.

Envoys from almost every part of Gaul, the leading men of their respective tribes, convened a camp to congratulate Caesar. They were aware, they said, that, if he had exacted atonement from the Helvetii by the sword for the wrongs they had done in the past to the Roman People, yet his action was just as much to the advantage of Gaul as of the Romans; for, though the Helvetii were perfectly well off, they had quitted their own abode with the intention of attacking the whole of Gaul, usurping dominion, selecting for occupation out of numerous tracts the one which they deemed the most suitable and the most fertile in the whole country, and making the other tribes their tributaries. The envoys begged to be allowed to convene, with Caesar's express sanction, a Pan-Gallic council for a particular day, representing that they had certain favors to ask of him after their substance was unanimously agreed upon. Their request being granted, they fixed a date for the council, and bound themselves mutually by oath not to disclose its proceedings without official sanction.

After the council had broken up, the tribal leaders who had been closeted with Caesar before returned, and asked permission to discuss with him privately, in a place secluded from observation, matters which concerned their own and the common weal. Their request being acceded to, they all prostrated themselves with tears at Caesar's feet. They told him that it was their aim and endeavor to prevent what they said from being disclosed no less than to obtain the favors they desired; because they saw that if it were disclosed, they would incur the most cruel punishment. Their spokesman was the Aeduan Diviciacus. Gaul, he said, comprised, as a whole, two rival groups, the Aedui being the overlords of one and the Arverni of the other. The two tribes had been struggling hard for supremacy for many years, when it happened that the Arverni and the Sequani hired Germans to join them. About fifteen thousand had crossed the Rhine in the first instance; but the rude barbarians conceived a passion for the lands, the civilization, and the wealth of the Gauls, and afterwards more crossed over, the number at that time in Gaul amounting to twenty thousand. The Aedui and their dependents had encountered them repeatedly, had been beaten, and had suffered a great disaster, losing all their men of rank, all their council, and all their knighthood. Overwhelmed by these disastrous defeats, they, whose prowess and whose hospitable and amicable relations with the Roman People had before made them supreme in Gaul, had been forced to give as hostages to the Sequani their most illustrious citizens, and to bind the tribe by oath not to attempt to recover the hostages, or to solicit aid from the Roman People, and to remain forever without demur beneath the sovereign power of their conquerors. He himself was the only man of the whole Aeduan community who could not be prevailed upon to take the oath or to give his children as hostages. He had therefore fled from his country and gone to Rome to claim assistance from the Senate, because he alone was not bound either by oath or surrender of hostages. A worse fate, however, had befallen the victorious Sequani than the beaten Aedui, for Ariovistus, king of the Germans, had settled in their country and seized one-third of the Sequanian territory,—the best land in the whole of Gaul; and now he insisted that the Sequani should quit another third, because a few months previously twenty-four thousand Harudes had joined him, and he had to find a place for them to settle in. Within a few years the whole population of Gaul would be expatriated, and the Germans would all cross the Rhine; for there was no comparison between the land of the Gauls and that of the Germans, or between the standard of living of the former and that of the latter. Ariovistus, having defeated the united Gallic forces in one battle, which took place at Magetobriga, was exercising his authority with arrogance and cruelty, demanding from every man of rank his children as hostages, and inflicting upon them all kinds of cruel punishments if the least intimation of his will were not obeyed. The man was a ferocious headstrong savage; and it was impossible to endure his dictation any longer. Unless Caesar and the Roman People could help them, the Gauls must all do as the Helvetii had done,—leave house and home, seek another abode, other settlements out of reach of the Germans, and take their chance of whatever might befall them. If his words were reported to Ariovistus, he had no doubt that he would inflict the heaviest penalty upon all the hostages in his keeping. Caesar, by his prestige and that of his army, or by his late victory, or by the weight of the Roman name, could deter any fresh host of Germans from crossing the Rhine, and protect the whole of Gaul from the outrageous conduct of Ariovistus.

After Diviciacus had made this speech, all who were present began to weep bitterly and to entreat Caesar for help. He noticed that the Sequani alone did not behave like the rest, but remained mournfully looking down, with heads bowed. In astonishment he asked them what was the reason of this behavior. The Sequani made no reply, but remained, without uttering, in the same mournful mood. After he had questioned them repeatedly without being able to get a single word out of them, the Aeduan, Diviciacus, again answered: the lot of the Sequani, he explained, was more pitiable and more grievous than that of the others, because they alone dared not, even in secret, complain or implore help; and though Ariovistus was away, they dreaded his cruelty just as much as if he were there, confronting them; for, while the others had at any rate the chance of escape, the Sequani, having admitted Ariovistus within their territories, and all their strongholds being in his power, would have to submit to every form of cruel punishment.

On learning these facts, Caesar reassured the Gauls and promised to give the matter his attention, remarking that he had every hope that Ariovistus, in return for his kindness and in deference to his authority, would cease his outrages. When he had finished speaking, he dismissed the assembly. Besides these considerations, indeed, many circumstances forced upon him the conviction that this problem must be faced and solved. First of all, there was the fact that the Aedui, who had repeatedly been recognized as Brethren, indeed kinsmen, by the Senate, were held in subjection under the sway of the Germans, while their hostages, as he knew, were detained by Ariovistus and the Sequani; and this, considering the great power of the Roman People, he regarded as an extreme disgrace to himself and his country. Besides, that the Germans should insensibly form the habit of crossing the Rhine, and enter Gaul in large numbers was, he saw, fraught with danger to the Roman People. He believed, too, that, being fierce barbarians, they would not stop short when they had taken possession of the whole of Gaul, but would pass into the Province, as the Cimbri and Teutoni had done before them, and thence push on into Italy, especially as the Sequani were only separated from our Province by the Rhone; and he thought it essential to obviate this danger at the earliest possible moment. Moreover, Ariovistus himself had assumed an inflated and arrogant demeanor, which made him quite insufferable.

Accordingly Caesar decided to send envoys to Ariovistus, requesting him to name some spot, midway between their respective quarters, for a proposal for conference, and saying that he wished to discuss with him political affairs and matters of the utmost importance to both parties. Ariovistus told the envoys in reply that, if he had wanted anything from Caesar, he would have gone to him in person, and if Caesar wanted anything from him, he must come to him. Besides, he could not venture to go without his army into the districts occupied by Caesar, and he could not concentrate his army without collecting a large quantity of stores, which would involve great labour. Moreover, he was at a loss to understand what business Caesar, or for that matter the Roman People, had in his part of Gaul, which he had conquered by the sword.

When this reply was conveyed to Caesar, he again sent envoys to Ariovistus with the following message:—Ariovistus had been treated with great kindness by himself and by the Roman People, having, in his consulship, received from the Senate the titles of King and Friend. Since he showed his gratitude to himself and the Roman People by raising objections when invited to a conference, and refusing to make any statement or to inform himself about matters which concerned them both, these were Caesar's demands:— first, he must not bring any additional body of men across the Rhine into Gaul; secondly, he must restore the hostages belonging to the Aedui, and authorize the Sequani to restore theirs; furthermore, he must not provoke the Aedui by outrages or attack them or their allies. If he complied, Caesar and the Roman People would be bound to him by lasting goodwill and amity. If not, then, in accordance with the resolution which the Senate had passed in the consulship of Marcus Messala and Marcus Piso—that the Governor of Gaul for the time being should, so far as the public interest would permit, protect the Aedui and the other friends of the Roman People—Caesar would not suffer the wrongs of the Aedui to go unavenged.

Ariovistus replied that the rights of war entitled conquerors to dictate their own terms to the conquered. The Roman People acted on the same principle: they regularly dealt with conquered peoples, not in obedience to the mandate of a third party, but according to their own judgement. If he did not dictate to the Roman People how they should exercise their rights, the Roman People ought not to interfere with him in the exercise of his. The Aedui had become his tributaries because they tempted the fortune of war, fought, and suffered defeat. Caesar was doing him a serious injury; for his coming depreciated the tribute. He would not restore the Aedui their hostages; but neither would he attack them or their allies wantonly if they abided by their agreement and paid their tribute annually. If not, much good would the title of "Brethren of the Roman People" do them! As for Caesar's threat, that he would not suffer the wrongs of the Aedui to go unavenged, no man had ever fought Ariovistus and escaped destruction. Let Caesar come on when he liked: he would then appreciate the mettle of Germans who had never known defeat, whose lives had been passed in war, and who, for fourteen years, had never sheltered beneath a roof.

Simultaneously with the delivery of this message envoys came to Caesar from the Aedui against Ario and the Treveri; the Aedui to complain that the Harudes, who had recently migrated into Gaul, were devastating their territory, and that even the surrender of hostages had failed to purchase the forbearance of Ariovistus, while the Treveri announced that one hundred clans of the Suevi, commanded by two brothers, Nasua and Cimberius, had established themselves on the banks of the Rhine, intending to attempt a passage. Caesar was seriously alarmed. He considered it necessary to act at once, lest, if a fresh horde of Suevi joined Ariovistus's veteran force, it might be harder to cope with him. Accordingly he arranged as quickly as possible for a supply of grain, and advanced against Ariovistus by forced marches.

After a march of three days he received news that Ariovistus was hurrying with all his forces to seize Vesontio, the largest town of the Sequani, and had advanced three days' journey beyond his own frontier. Caesar felt it necessary to make a great effort to forestall him, for the town was well provided with military material of every kind; and its natural strength made it a most valuable military position, the river Doubs winding round in a course that might have been traced with a compass, and almost surrounding the stronghold. The remaining space, not more than sixteen hundred feet, where the river left a gap, was occupied by a hill of great elevation, the banks of the river on either side touching the base of the hill. The hill itself was converted into a citadel by a wall, which surrounded it and connected it with the town. Caesar pushed on by forced marches night and day, took possession of, and garrisoned the town. While he was halting for a few days to collect corn and other supplies, a violent panic suddenly seized the whole army, completely paralyzing every one's judgement and nerve. It arose from the inquisitiveness of our men and the chatter of the Gauls and the traders, who affirmed that the Germans were men of huge stature, incredible valour, and practiced skill in war: many a time they had themselves come across them, and had not been able even to look them in the face or meet the glare of their piercing eyes. The panic began with the tribunes, the auxiliary officers, and others who had left the capital to follow Caesar in the hope of winning his favor, and had little experience in war. Some of them applied for leave of absence, alleging various urgent reasons for their departure, though a good many, anxious to avoid the imputation of cowardice, stayed behind for very shame. They were unable, however, to assume an air of unconcern, and sometimes even to restrain their tears; shutting themselves up in their tents, they bemoaned their own fate or talked dolefully with their intimates of the peril that threatened the army. All over the camp men were making their wills. Gradually even legionaries, centurions, and cavalry officers, who had long experience of campaigning, were unnerved by these alarmists. Those who did not want to be thought cowards said that it was not the enemy they were afraid of, but the narrow roads and the huge forests which separated them from Ariovistus, or the difficulty of bringing up grain. Some actually told Caesar that when he gave the order to strike the camp and advance, the men would not obey, and would be too terrified to move.

Observing the state of affairs, Caesar called a meeting, to which the centurions of all offices and grades were summoned, and rated them severely for presuming to suppose that it was their business to inquire or even to consider where they were going, or on what errand. When he was consul, Ariovistus had eagerly solicited the friendship of the Roman People. Why, then, should any one suppose that he would abandon his loyal attitude in this hare-brained way? For his own part, he was convinced that when he came to know his demands and realized the fairness of his terms, he would not reject his friendship or that of the Roman People. But supposing he were carried away by mad passion and went to war, what on earth was there to fear? Or why should they distrust their own courage or his generalship? The measure of their enemy had been taken at a time which their fathers could remember, when the Cimbri and Teutoni were defeated by Gaius Marius, and the army confessedly earned no less credit than their commander; and again in recent years in Italy during the Slave War, although the slaves were, in some measure, helped by the experience and discipline which they had learned from us. This war enabled one to appreciate the value of steadfastness; for the men whom the Romans had long dreaded without reason, while they were without arms, they afterwards overcame when they were armed and flushed with victory. Finally, these Germans were the same whom the Helvetii had many times encountered, not only in their own but in German territory, and generally beaten: yet the Helvetii were no match for our army. Those who were alarmed by the defeat and rout of the Gauls could ascertain, if they inquired, that the Gauls were tired out by the long duration of the war, and that Ariovistus, after keeping himself shut up for many months in an encampment protected by marshes without giving them a chance of attacking him, suddenly fell upon them when they had dispersed in despair of bringing him to action, and beat them by craft and stratagem rather than by valour. Ariovistus himself could not expect that Roman armies were to be trapped by the craft for which there had been an opening against the simple natives. Those who pretended that their cowardice was only anxiety about supplies and the narrow roads were guilty of presumption; for it was evident that they either had no confidence in their general's sense of duty or meant to lecture him. These things were his business. The Sequani, the Leuci, and the Lingones were providing grain, and the corn in the fields was already ripe: about the road they would shortly judge for themselves. As to the report that they did not intend to obey orders and advance, that did not trouble him at all; for he knew that generals whose armies mutinied were either bunglers whose luck had deserted them, or had been detected in some scandalous crime, and thereby convicted of avarice. The whole tenor of his life proved his integrity, and the war with the Helvetii his good fortune. Accordingly he intended to do at once what he would otherwise have postponed: on the following night, in the fourth watch, he should strike his camp, so as to find out as soon as possible whether honor and duty or cowardice were the stronger motive with them. If no one else would follow him, he would go on alone with the 10th legion, in which he had full confidence; and it should be his bodyguard. This legion Caesar had always treated with special favor, and, on account of its soldierly spirit, he trusted it in the highest degree.

After this speech a marvelous change came over the temper of all ranks, and the utmost of them. The 10th legion, taking the initiative, miles away from them, conveyed their thanks to Caesar through their tribunes for having expressed such a high opinion of them, and declared themselves perfectly ready to take the field. Following their lead, the other legions deputed their tribunes and chief centurions to make their apologies to Caesar, protesting that they had never hesitated or been afraid, and that they recognized that it was the general's business and not theirs to direct the campaign. Their excuses were accepted. By the aid of Diviciacus, in whom he had more confidence than in any of the other Gauls, Caesar had discovered a route which, though it would involve making a detour of more than fifty miles, would enable him to march through open country. He kept his word, and started in the fourth watch. After a continuous march of seven days, he was informed by his patrols that Ariovistus's forces were twenty-four miles from ours.

On learning of Caesar's arrival, Ariovistus sent envoys to say that, since he had come nearer, and his own safety would probably not be imperiled, he would not oppose his original request for an interview. Caesar did not spurn his offer, believing that he was now returning to reason, as he offered, of his own accord, to do what he had refused before when he was asked; and he entertained a strong hope that when he learned his demands, he would, in consideration of the great favors conferred upon him by himself and the Roman People, abandon his stubborn attitude.

The interview was fixed for the fourth day following. Meanwhile envoys were frequently passing to and fro between the two generals. Ariovistus insisted that Caesar should not bring any infantry to the conference, as he was afraid he might treacherously surround him; they must each come with a mounted escort, otherwise he would not come at all. Caesar, not wishing any obstacle to stand in the way and stop the conference, and fearing to trust his life to Gallic cavalry, decided that his best plan would be to dismount all the Gallic troopers and mount the infantry of the 10th legion, in whom he had the greatest confidence, on their horses, so that, in case it were necessary to act, he might have an escort on whose devotion he could absolutely rely. On this, one of the soldiers of the 10th remarked with a touch of humour, "Caesar is better than his word; he promised to make the 10th his bodyguard, and now he's knighting us."

There was a great plain, in which was an earthen mound of considerable size about equidistant from the camps of Ariovistus and of Caesar. To this spot they came, as agreed, to hold the conference. Caesar posted the mounted legion, which he had brought with him, four hundred paces from the mound; and Ariovistus's horsemen took up a position at the same distance. Ariovistus stipulated that he and Caesar should confer on horseback, each accompanied by ten men. When they reached the spot Caesar began by recalling the kindness with which he himself and the Senate had treated Ariovistus—the Senate had conferred upon him the titles of Wing and Friend, and the handsomest presents had been sent to him. Such a mark of favor, he told him, had fallen to the lot of few, and was usually bestowed only as a reward for great services. Ariovistus had no right to approach the Senate and no title to claim anything; and it was to the kindness and generosity of himself and the Senate that he owed these distinctions. Caesar explained further that between the Romans and the Aedui there were longstanding and solid grounds of intimacy; senatorial resolutions, couched in the most complimentary terms, had repeatedly been passed in their favor, and at all times, even before they sought our friendship, the Aedui had held the foremost position in the whole of Gaul! As a matter of settled policy, the Roman People desired their allies and friends not only to lose nothing by the connection, but to be gainers in influence, dignity, and consideration; who, then, could suffer them to be robbed of what they already possessed when they sought the friendship of the Roman People? Caesar then repeated the demands which he had charged his envoys to present,—that Ariovistus should not make war upon the Aedui or upon their allies; that he should restore the hostages; and that, if he were unable to send back any of the Germans to their own country, he should at all events not suffer any more to cross the Rhine.

Ariovistus said little in reply to Caesar's demands, but spoke at great length about his own merits. He said that he had not crossed the Rhine spontaneously, but in response to the urgent request of the Gauls; he had not left home and kinsmen without great expectations and great inducements; the possessions which he occupied in Gaul had been ceded to him by Gauls; their hostages had been given voluntarily; while by the rights of war he made them pay the tribute which conquerors habitually exacted from the conquered. He had not made war upon the Gauls; the Gauls had made war upon him. The tribes of Gaul had all come to attack him, and kept the field against him; and he had beaten the whole host in a single battle and crushed them. If they wanted to try again, he was ready for another fight; if they wanted peace, it was not fair of them to refuse their tribute, which they had hitherto paid of their own free will. The friendship of the Roman People ought to be a distinction and a protection, not a drawback; and it was with that expectation that he had sought it. If through their interference his tribute were stopped and those who had surrendered to him withdrawn from his control, he would be just as ready to discard their friendship as he had been to ask for it. If he continued to bring Germans in large numbers into Gaul, he did so not for aggression but in self-defense; the proof was that he had not come till he was asked, and that he had not attacked but only repelled attack. He had come to Gaul before the Romans. Never till now had a Roman army stirred outside the frontier of the Province of Gaul. What did Caesar mean by invading his dominions? This part of Gaul was his province, just as the other was ours. If he made a raid into our territory, we should be wrong to give in to him; similarly, it was unjust of us to obstruct him in his rightful sphere. Caesar said that the Aedui had been given the title of Brethren by the Senate; but he was not such an oaf, he was not so ignorant of the world as not to know that in the late war with the Allobroges the Aedui had not helped the Romans, and that in the struggle which the Aedui had had with himself and the Sequani, they had not had the benefit of Roman aid. He was bound to suspect that Caesar, under the mask of friendship, was keeping his army in Gaul to ruin him. Unless he took his departure and withdrew his army from the neighborhood, he should treat him not as a friend but as an enemy; in fact, if he put him to death, he should be doing an acceptable service to many of the nobles and leading men of Rome. This he knew as a fact, for he had it through their agents from their own lips; and he could purchase the gratitude and friendship of them all by killing him. If, on the other hand, he withdrew and left him in undisturbed possession of Gaul, he would reward him handsomely; and whenever he had occasion to go to war, he would fight all his battles for him and save him all trouble and risk.

Caesar spoke at considerable length, the gist of his speech being that he could not abandon his undertaking; that his own principles and those of the Roman People would not allow him to forsake deserving allies; and that he could not admit that Gaul belonged to Ariovistus any more than to the Roman People. The Arverni and the Ruteni had been conquered by Quintus Fabius Maximus; but the Roman People had granted them an amnesty, and had not annexed their country or imposed tribute upon them. If priority of occupation were to be considered, the title of the Roman People to dominion in Gaul was unimpeachable; if they were to abide by the decision of the Senate, Gaul had a right to independence, for the Senate, although it had conquered Gaul, had granted it autonomy.

While these questions were being argued Caesar was informed that Ariovistus's horsemen were moving nearer the mound, riding towards the conference and our men and throwing stones and other missiles at them. Caesar ceased speaking, went back to his men, and ordered them not to retaliate; for although he saw that the legion of his choice would run no risk in engaging the cavalry, he did not choose, by beating the enemy, to let it be said that he had pledged his word and then surrounded them while a conference was going on. When the news spread to the ranks that Ariovistus, in the course of the conference, had arrogantly denied the right of the Romans to be in Gaul, and that his cavalry had attacked our troops, thereby breaking off the conference, the army was inspired with a more intense enthusiasm and eagerness for battle.

Two days later Ariovistus sent envoys to Caesar, saying that he desired to confer with him on the questions which they had begun to discuss without reaching any conclusion: let Caesar confer with Ariovistus, either name another day for a conference, or, if he were disinclined to do that, send one of his men to represent him. Caesar saw no reason for further discussion, especially as on the preceding day the Germans could not be prevented from throwing missiles at our men; while to send a representative would be very dangerous, and would be placing him at the mercy of savages. The best course appeared to be to send Gaius Valerius Procillus, son of Gaius Valerius Caburus, a young man of the highest character and a true gentleman, whose father had been enfranchised by Gaius Valerius Flaccus. He selected him because he could be thoroughly trusted, and because he knew Gallic, which Ariovistus, from long practice, now spoke fluently, and also because, in his case, the Germans had no motive for foul play. With him he sent Marcus Metius, who was on friendly terms with Ariovistus. Their instructions were to hear what Ariovistus had to say and report to him. When Ariovistus caught sight of them, close by, in his camp, he roared out before the troops, "What are you coming to me for? To play the spy?" When they attempted to speak, he silenced them and put them in irons.

On the same day he advanced and took a position six miles from Caesar's camp, at the foot of a hill. The following day he marched his force past Caesar's camp and encamped two miles beyond, with the intention of cutting him off from the corn and other supplies which were being brought up from the territories of the Sequani and the Aedui. On each of the five following days Caesar regularly led out his troops in front of his camp, and kept them in line of battle, to give Ariovistus the chance of fighting if he wished. During all this time Ariovistus kept his army shut up in camp, but skirmished daily with his cavalry. The mode of fighting practiced by the Germans was as follows. They had six thousand cavalry, with the same number of infantry, swift runners of extraordinary courage, each one of whom had been selected by one of the cavalry out of the whole host for his own protection. The cavalry were accompanied by them in action, and regularly fell back upon their support. In case of a check, they flocked to the rescue; whenever a trooper was severely wounded and fell from his horse, they rallied round him; and they had acquired such speed by training that if it was necessary to make a forced march or retreat rapidly, they supported themselves by the horses' manes and kept pace with them.

Seeing that Ariovistus meant to keep Caesar within his camp, and being resolved to reopen communication with his envoys without delay, Caesar selected a suitable position for a camp about twelve hundred paces beyond the spot where the Germans were encamped, and advanced to this position in three columns. Keeping the first and second under arms, he ordered the third to construct a camp. The site, as I have said, was about twelve hundred paces from the enemy. Ariovistus sent about sixteen thousand light infantry with all his cavalry to overawe our men and prevent them from completing the entrenchment. Nevertheless, Caesar, adhering to his original resolve, ordered the first two lines to keep the enemy at bay, while the third finished the entrenchment. When the camp was entrenched, he left two legions and a detachment of auxiliaries to hold it, and withdrew the remaining four to the larger camp.

The next day Caesar, according to his regular superstition practice, made his troops move out of both camps, and, advancing a short distance from the larger one, formed a line of battle and gave the enemy an opening for attack. Seeing that they would not come out even then, he withdrew his army into camp about midday. Then at last Ariovistus sent a detachment to attack the smaller camp. Fighting was kept up with spirit on both sides till evening. At sunset Ariovistus led back his forces, which had inflicted heavy loss upon the Romans and suffered heavily themselves, into camp. On inquiring from prisoners why he would not fight a decisive battle, Caesar found that the reason was this:—among the Germans it was customary for the matrons to tell by lots and divinations whether it would be advantageous to fight or not, and their decision was that it was not fated that the Germans should gain the victory if they fought before the new moon.

Next day Caesar left detachments of adequate strength to guard the two camps; posted all his auxiliaries, in view of the enemy, in front of the smaller one, with the object of creating a moral effect, as his regular infantry, compared with the enemy, were numerically rather weak; and, forming his army in three lines, advanced right up to the enemy's camp. Then at last the Germans perforce led their troops out of camp, formed them up at equal intervals in tribal groups—Harudes, Marcomanni, Triboci, Vangiones, Nemetes, Sedusii, and Suevi—and closed their whole line with wagons and carts, to do away with all hope of escape. In the wagons they placed their women, who, as they were marching out to battle, stretched out their hands and besought them with tears not to deliver them into bondage to the Romans. Caesar placed each of his generals and his quaestor in command of a legion, so that every man might feel that his courage would be recognized, and engaged with the right wing, which he commanded in person, for he observed that the troops which faced it were the weakest part of the enemy's line. When the signal was given, our men charged the enemy with such vigor, and the enemy dashed forward so suddenly and so swiftly that there was no time to hurl the javelins at them. The men therefore dropped their javelins and fought hand to hand with swords. The Germans, however, rapidly formed in a phalanx—their usual order—and thus sustained the impact of the swords. Many of our men actually leaped on to the phalanx, tore the shields out of their enemies' hands, and stabbed them from above. On the left wing the enemy's line was beaten and put to flight; but on the right their great numbers enabled them to press our line very hard. Noticing this, the younger Publius Crassus, who commanded the cavalry, and was more free to observe and act than the officers who were engaged in the actual fighting, sent the third line to the relief of our hard-pressed troops.

Thus the battle was restored, and the enemy all turned tail and did not cease their flight until they reached the Rhine, about five miles from the battlefield. A few, trusting to their strong limbs, struck out and swam across; a few found boats and saved themselves. Among the latter was Ariovistus, who found a skiff moored by the bank, and escaped in it. All the rest were hunted down by our cavalry and slain. Ariovistus had two wives, one a Suevan by birth, whom he had brought with him from his own country, the other a Norican, a sister of King Voccio, who had been sent to him by her brother, and whom he had married in Gaul. Both of them perished in the rout. He also had two daughters, one of whom was killed and the other captured. Gaius Valerius Procillus was being dragged along among the fugitives by his warders, fettered with three chains, when he fell in with Caesar, who was leading the cavalry in pursuit of the enemy. To see this excellent Provincial, his own familiar friend, rescued from the enemy's clutches and restored to him, and to feel that Fortune had not brought upon him any calamity that could lessen the pleasure of a victory upon which he might fairly congratulate himself—these things gave Caesar no less pleasure than the victory itself. Procillus said that, in his own presence, they had cast lots three times to see whether he should be burned alive at once or kept for execution later; and happily the lots had so fallen that he was safe. Marcus Metius also was found and brought back to Caesar.

When the result of the battle was known beyond the Rhine, the Suevi, who had reached the banks of the river, turned homewards. The Ubii, who live in the immediate neighborhood of the Rhine, seeing their alarm, pursued them and killed a large number. Having finished two important campaigns in a single summer, Caesar led his army back to winter in the country of the Sequani a little before the usual time, and, placing Labienus in command of the camp, started for Cisalpine Gaul to hold the assizes.

BOOK II

The First Campaign against the Belgae

While Caesar, as we have mentioned above, was in Cisalpine Gaul, frequent rumors reached him, which were confirmed by dispatches from Labienus, that the Belgae, whose territory, as we have remarked, forms a third part of Gaul, were all conspiring against the Roman People and exchanging hostages. The motives of the conspiracy, it appeared, were these: first, the Belgae were afraid that, as the whole of Gaul was tranquillized, our army might advance against them. Secondly, they were egged on by sundry Gauls, some of whom, just as they had objected to the continued presence of the Germans in Gaul, were irritated by the Roman army wintering in the country and settling there, while others, from instability and fickleness of temperament, hankered after a change of masters; and also by powerful individuals, especially those who had the means of hiring mercenaries, who, as often happened in Gaul, had been wont to usurp royal authority, and found it less easy to achieve this end under our dominion.

Alarmed by these messages and dispatches Caesar raised two new legions in Cisalpine Gaul and directed Quintus Pedius, one of his generals, to lead them, at the beginning of the fine weather, into Further Gaul. As soon as forage began to be plentiful he joined the army in person, and charged the Senones and the other Gauls who were conterminous with the Belgae to find out what was going on in their country and keep him informed. They all agreed in reporting that levies were being raised and that an army was concentrating. Caesar now thought it his duty to march against them without hesitation. After arranging for a supply of grain, he broke up his camp and reached the Belgic frontier in about a fortnight.

He arrived unexpectedly and sooner than anyone had anticipated. The Remi—the nearest of the Belgae to Gaul—sent Iccius and Andecumborius, the leading men of the tribe, as envoys, to say that they would place their lives and all that they possessed under the protection and at the disposal of the Roman People; that they had not shared the counsels of the other Belgae or joined their conspiracy against the Roman People, and that they were prepared to give hostages, to obey orders, to admit the Romans into their strongholds, and to supply them with corn and other necessaries; that all the other Belgae were in arms, and that the Germans who dwelt on the near side of the Rhine had joined them; and that they were all possessed by such frenzy that the Remi could not deter even the Suessiones, their own kith and kin, who had the same rights and laws as themselves, and jointly owned the authority of one and the same magistrate, from taking their side.

On inquiring from the envoys the names of the belligerent tribes, their size, and their military strength, Caesar collected the following information. Most of the Belgae were of German origin, and had crossed the Rhine at a remote period and settled in Gaul on account of the fertility of the land. They had driven out the Gallic inhabitants, and were the only people who, at the time within the memory of our fathers, when the whole of Gaul was devastated, prevented the Teutoni and the Cimbri from invading their country. Inspired by the memory of that achievement, they arrogated to themselves great authority, and assumed the air of a great military power. With regard to their numbers the Remi professed to have full information, for, being allied to them by blood and intermarriage, they had ascertained the strength of the contingent which each tribe had promised in the general counsel of the Belgae for the impending war. The Bellovaci, who, from their valour, prestige, and numbers, were the most powerful of all, and could muster one hundred thousand armed men, had promised sixty thousand picked troops, and claimed the general direction of the campaign. The Suessiones were their own neighbors, and their territory was very extensive and very fertile. Within the memory of men still living, their king had been Diviciacus, the most powerful prince in the whole of Gaul, who was overlord not only of a large part of the Belgic territory, but also of Britain. The reigning king was Galba, who, on account of his integrity and sound judgement, was unanimously entrusted with the chief command. The Suessiones possessed twelve strongholds, and promised fifty thousand armed men. The same number was promised by the Nervii, who were considered by the Belgae themselves as the fiercest of them all, and who were the most remote. The Atrebates promised fifteen thousand; the Ambiani ten thousand; the Menapii seven thousand; the Caleti ten thousand; the Veliocasses and the Viromandui jointly the same number; the Aduatuci nineteen thousand; the Condrusi, the Eburones, the Caeroesi, and the Paemani (who are known by the common appellation of Germans promised), so the Remi believed, about forty thousand.

Caesar addressed the Remi in encouraging and gracious terms, and ordered their entire council to meet him and the children of the leading men to be brought to him as hostages. All these orders they carefully and punctually obeyed. He then earnestly impressed upon the Aeduan, Diviciacus, that it was most important, in the interest of the Republic, and indeed of Aeduans and Romans alike, to break up the enemy's forces, so as to avoid the necessity of engaging such a powerful host at once. The object could be attained if the Aedui marched into the country of the Bellovaci and proceeded to devastate their lands. With this injunction he dismissed Diviciacus. Finding that all the Belgic forces had concentrated and were marching against him, and learning from the reconnoitering parties which he had sent out and from the Remi that they were now not far off, he pushed on rapidly, crossed the Aisne, which flows through the most distant part of the country of the Remi, and encamped near its banks. This movement northern protected one side of his camp by the banks of the river, secured his rear, and enabled his supplies to be brought up without danger by the Remi and the other tribes. The river was spanned by a bridge, at the head of which he established a strong post, while on the other side of the river he left six cohorts under one of his generals, Titurius Sabinus. At the same time he ordered a camp to be constructed, with a rampart twelve feet high and a trench eighteen feet wide.

Eight miles from the camp there was a town belonging to the Remi called Bibrax. The Rax! Belgae attacked it furiously on their march; and the garrison had difficulty in holding out that day. The following method of attacking forts is practiced by Gauls and Belgae alike. Surrounding the whole circuit of the fortifications with a multitude of men, they proceed to hurl stones from all sides against the wall, and when they have cleared it, they lock their shields over their heads, advance right up to the gates, and undermine the wall. In this case the operation was easily performed, for with such a huge host hurling stones and other missiles no man had a chance of keeping his footing on the wall. When night stopped the attack, Iccius, a Roman of the highest rank, and very popular with his countrymen, who was acting as governor of the town, one of the envoys who had come to Caesar to sue for peace, sent him word that, unless a force were sent to his relief, he could hold out no longer.

About midnight Caesar, employing as guides the messengers who had come from Diviciacus, sent Numidian and Cretan archers and Balearic slingers to Bibrax, to relieve the inhabitants. On their arrival, the Remi, inspired by the hope of repelling the attack, became eager to take the offensive; and for the same reason the enemy abandoned the hope of taking the town. Accordingly, after lingering a short time in the neighborhood, ravaging the lands of the Remi, and burning all the villages and homesteads within reach, they pushed on with all their forces towards Caesar's camp, and encamped barely two miles off. Judging by the smoke and watch-fires, their camp extended more than eight miles in width. Caesar determined, in the first instance, to avoid an action, on account of the great numbers of the enemy and of their extraordinary reputation for valour: still, he daily tested the mettle of the enemy and the daring of our troops, and found that the latter were a match for them. The ground in front of his camp was naturally just suited for forming a line of battle. The hill on which the camp stood, rising gradually from the plain, extended, facing the enemy, over the exact space which the line would occupy: on either flank its sides descended abruptly, while in front it gradually merged in the plain by a gentle slope. On either side of the hill Caesar drew a trench athwart, about eight hundred paces long, and at the end of each trench erected a redoubt, in which he posted artillery to prevent the enemy, when he had formed his line, from taking advantage of their great numerical superiority to attack his men in flank and surround them. Having done this, he left his two newly-raised legions in camp, so that they might be available at any point as a reserve, and drew up the remaining six in line of battle in front of the camp. The enemy likewise had marched their forces out of camp and formed them in line.

There was a morass of no great size between our army and that of the enemy. The ford the enemy waited to see whether our men would order to cross it; while our men, weapons in hand, were Caesar's ready to attack them in case they crossed first, when their movements would be impeded. Meanwhile a skirmish of horse was going on between the two lines. Neither side would cross first, and, the skirmish resulting in favor of our men, Caesar withdrew his infantry into camp. Forthwith the enemy moved rapidly from their position to gain the river Aisne, which, as the narrative has shown, was in the rear of our camp. There they discovered a ford, and endeavored to throw a part of their force across, intending, if possible, to storm the redoubt commanded by the general, Quintus Titurius, and break down the bridge; or, failing this, to devastate the lands of the Remi, who were very useful to us in the campaign, and to cut off our troops from supplies.

Caesar, on receiving information from Titurius, took the whole of his cavalry, his light-armed Numidians, slingers, and archers across the bridge, and pushed on rapidly against them.

A fierce combat took place at the spot where they were crossing. Our men attacked the enemy in the river, while their movements were impeded, and killed a great number of them: the rest made a most daring attempt to get across over their dead bodies, but were beaten back by a shower of missiles; while the leading division, who had crossed already, were surrounded by the cavalry and killed. The enemy realized that they had deceived themselves in expecting to storm the stronghold and cross the river: they saw that the Romans would not advance and fight on an unfavorable position; and their supply of grain was beginning to run short. They therefore called a council of war, and decided that the best course would be for the several contingents to return home, and rally from all parts to the defense of the people whose country the Roman army invaded first: they would thus fight in their own and not in foreign territory, and have the benefit of homegrown supplies. Among other reasons, they were led to adopt this resolution by the knowledge that Diviciacus and the Aedui were approaching the country of the Bellovaci, and the latter could not be induced to remain any longer and refrain from helping their own people.

Their departure resembled a rout. Caesar was promptly informed of what they had done by scouts. Fearing an ambuscade (for he did not yet clearly see the reason for their departure), he kept his army, including the cavalry, in camp. At daybreak the report was confirmed by patrols; and Caesar sent on ahead the whole of his cavalry, commanded by two generals, Quintus Pedius and Lucius Aurunculeius Cotta, to retard the rearguard, at the same time ordering Titus Labienus to follow in support with three legions. This force attacked the rearguard and pursued them for many miles, killing a large number of the fugitives; for while the rearmost ranks, when overtaken, made a stand and gallantly resisted the attack of our infantry, the van, fancying themselves out of reach of danger and not being restrained by necessity or discipline, broke their ranks when they heard the distant cries and ran for their lives. Thus our men slaughtered them in numbers, without any risk to themselves, as long as daylight lasted: towards sunset they left off, and returned, in obedience to instructions, to camp.

On the day following, before the enemy could recover from their panic flight, Caesar led the army into the country of the Suessiones, who were conterminous with the Kemi, and Noviodu of Noviodunum. Hearing that it was undefended, he attempted, immediately after his arrival, to storm it; but the moat was so broad and the wall so high that, notwithstanding the small numbers of the garrison, he was unable to carry the position. After entrenching his camp, he proceeded to form a line of sheds, and to make the necessary preparations, for a siege. On the following night, before he could resume operations, the whole host of the fugitive Suessiones thronged into the town. The sheds were speedily brought up, earth was shot and towers were erected; and the Gauls, alarmed by the magnitude of the works, which they had never seen or even heard of before, and also by the swift energy of the Romans, sent envoys to Caesar, proposing to surrender. The Remi interceded for their lives; and their prayer was granted.

Caesar took the leading men of the tribe, as well as two of King Galba's own sons, as hostages; and, after all the arms in the town had been delivered up, he accepted the surrender of the Suessiones, and marched into the country of the Bellovaci, who threw themselves with all their belongings into the stronghold of Bratuspantium. When Caesar and his army were about five miles off, the older men all came out, stretched out their hands to him, and declared that they were ready to place themselves under his protection and in his power, and that they were not in arms against the Roman People. In like manner, when he had approached the stronghold and was encamping on its outskirts, the women and children stretched out their hands from the wall in the native fashion, and begged the Romans for peace.

Diviciacus, who, after the retreat of the Belgae, had disbanded the Aeduan forces and returned to Caesar, interceded for the suppliants. The Bellovaci, he said, had at all times been dependents of the Aedui, and in amicable relations with them; but, at the instigation of their leaders, who said that the Aedui had been enslaved by Caesar and had to put up with ill-usage and insult of every kind, they had abandoned their connection with them and taken up arms against the Roman People. The ringleaders, realizing the magnitude of the disaster which they had brought upon their country, had escaped to Britain. Not only the Bellovaci, but also the Aedui on their behalf, would beg Caesar to treat them with the forbearance and humanity for which he was distinguished. By doing so he would increase the authority of the Aedui among the Belgae generally, for the Aedui commonly relied on their assistance and resources to carry on any wars in which they happened to be engaged.

Caesar said that he would spare their lives and take them under his protection out of respect for Diviciacus and the Aedui; but, as the tribe ranked high among the Belgae and had a very large population, he required six hundred hostages. After they had been delivered over and all the arms brought out of the town and piled, Caesar marched from Bratuspantium to the territory of the Ambiani, who surrendered unreservedly without delay. Their territory was conterminous with that of the Nervii. Caesar made inquiries about the character, manners, and customs of this people, and collected the following information. Traders were not allowed to enter their country; they would not permit the importation of anything in the shape of wine or other luxuries, believing that courage was enfeebled by these indulgences and manly vigor enervated; they were a fierce, brave people; and, railing at the other Belgae and accusing them of having surrendered to the Romans and made shipwreck of their ancestral valour, they vowed that they would not send envoys or accept peace on any terms. After marching for three days through their territory, Caesar learned from prisoners that Nervii had all encamped on the further side of a river called the Sambre, which was not more than ten miles from his camp, and were there awaiting the arrival of the Romans, along with their neighbors, the Atrebates and the Viromandui, both of whom they had persuaded to share with them the fortune of war. They were waiting for the force of the Aduatuci, which was marching to join them and they had hastily transferred their women and all who were disqualified by age for fighting to a spot which was rendered inaccessible for an army by marshes.

On learning this, Caesar sent on ahead a reconnoitering party and centurions to choose a good position for a camp. A considerable number of the Belgae who had surrendered and other Gauls had followed him, and were marching in his train. Some of them, as was afterwards ascertained from prisoners, having observed the order in which our army marched during the first three days, made their way to the Nervii in the night, and explained to them that each legion was followed by a great quantity of baggage, and that when the foremost legion reached camp and the rest were a long way off, there would be no difficulty in attacking it while the men were burdened with their packs: when it was beaten and its baggage plundered, the rest would not venture to make a stand. One circumstance favoured the plan recommended by the men who gave this information. In times past the Nervii, having no cavalry (to this day they pay no attention to that arm, their whole strength being in infantry), devised the following method of checking their neighbors' cavalry, when they made plundering raids into their territory. Lopping off the tops of young saplings and bending them over, so that their branches shot out thickly sideways, they planted brambles and briers between, the hedges thus formed making a barrier like a wall, which it was impossible not only to penetrate, but even to see through. As the march of our column was delayed by these obstacles, the Nervii felt that the proffered advice was worth following.

Caesar had sent on his cavalry in advance, and was following with all his forces; but the troops' column was formed on a different principle from that which the Belgae had described to the Nervii. Six of Caesar's legions, according to his usual practice when he was approaching an enemy, were advancing in light marching order; behind them was the baggage-train of the entire army, followed by the two newly-raised legions, which closed the rear and protected the baggage. Our cavalry, along with the slingers and archers, crossed the river and engaged the enemy's horse.

The latter fell back repeatedly into the woods on the support of their comrades, and again emerging, charged our men, who dared not pursue them, when they retreated, beyond the fringe of the open ground. Meanwhile the six legions which had come up first proceeded to entrench the camp along the lines which had been marked out.

The camp was almost certainly on the heights of Neuf-Mesnil, on the left bank of the Sambre, opposite the camp.

When the head of our baggage-train was ambushed in the woods—the moment which they had agreed upon for beginning the battle—suddenly, in the exact order in which, with mutual exhortations, they had formed their line within, the whole force darted forth and swooped down upon our cavalry. Sending them flying in disorder without an effort, they rushed down to the stream with such incredible swiftness that it seemed as if almost at the same instant they were at the woods, in the river, and now at sword's point with our men. As swiftly they pressed up the hill to attack our camp and the men who were engaged in entrenching it.

Caesar had to arrange everything at once,— the red flag, the signal for arming; sound the trumpet; recall the men from the trenches; send for those who had gone further afield in search of wood; form the line; harangue the troops; and give the signal for battle. Want of time and the enemy's onset prevented much of this from being done. Two things, however, served to lighten his difficulties,—first, the knowledge and experience of the soldiers, who, as seasoned campaigners, were able to decide for themselves what ought to be done as well as others could tell them; and secondly, the fact that he had forbidden his marshals to leave the works and their respective legions till the camp was entrenched. As the enemy were so close and coming up so fast, they did not wait for orders from Caesar, but made the arrangements which they thought right on their own responsibility.

Caesar, after giving indispensable orders, hurried down at haphazard to encourage the soldiers, and came to the 10th legion. He spoke briefly, merely urging the men to remember their ancient valour, keep cool, and sustain resolutely the enemy's rush; then, as the enemy were within range, he gave the signal for action. Going on to another part of the field to encourage the men, he found them already engaged. Time was so short, and the enemy were so ready and eager for battle that there was not a moment even for putting on helmets and pulling the covers off shields, much less for fitting on crests. Each man, as he came down from the trenches, fell in by the standard he first caught sight of, wherever he happened to find himself, not wishing to waste the time for action in looking for the men of his company.

The army was drawn up as well as time permitted, according to the requirements of the ground and the slope of the hill rather than the formation prescribed by tactical rules. The legions were separated and making head against the enemy at different points; while the view was interrupted, as we have explained before, by hedges of extraordinary thickness. It was therefore impossible to post reserves at fixed points, or to foresee what would be wanted at each and every part of the field; nor could one man give all the necessary orders. With such adverse conditions, then, the vicissitudes of fortune were naturally various.

The men of the 9th and 10th legions were posted on the left of the line. With a volley of javelins they drove the Atrebates—the division which they had encountered—who were breathless and tired from their rapid charge and enfeebled by wounds, from the high ground to the river, and when they attempted to cross, pressed after them sword in hand, and killed a great many while their movements were impeded. Crossing themselves without hesitation, and pushing on though the slope was against them, when the enemy rallied they renewed the combat and routed them. Similarly in another part of the field two legions, the 11th and 8th, which were separated from one another, encountered the Viromandui, drove them from the higher ground, and maintained the combat right on the banks of the river. Nearly the whole camp, however, in front and on the left, was exposed; and, the 12th legion and at no great distance the 7th being posted on the right wing, the whole of the Nervii, formed in a compact column and led by Boduognatus, the commander-in-chief, advanced rapidly against the position; and while some of them began to move round the legions on their exposed flank, others made for the summit of the hill, on which the camp stood.

At the same time our cavalry and the light-armed foot associated with them, who were routed, as I have said, by the enemy's first charge, were retreating to the camp, when they came full upon the enemy and again took to flight in another direction; and the servants, who from the rear-gate, situated on the crest of the ridge, had seen our victorious troops cross the river and had gone out to plunder, looked back and, seeing the enemy moving about in the camp, precipitately fled. Simultaneously a babel of voices arose from the men who were coming up with the baggage, and they rushed panic-stricken in different directions. A body of horsemen belonging to the Treveri, whose courage is proverbial among the Gauls, had been sent by their tribe, as an auxiliary force, to join Caesar. Alarmed by all these signs of panic, seeing that our camp was thronged by the enemy, that the legions were hard pressed and all but hemmed in, that servants, horsemen, slingers, and Numidians had parted company and scattered and were flying in all directions, they despaired of our success, hastened homewards, and told their countrymen that the Romans were disastrously defeated, and that the enemy had captured their camp and baggage.

Caesar, after haranguing the 10th legion, had gone off to the right wing. He saw that his troops were hard pressed and that the men of the 12th legion, their standards closely massed, were crowded together and preventing each other from fighting: all the centurions of the 4th cohort, as well as the standard-bearer, were killed; the standard was lost; almost all the centurions of the other cohorts were either killed or wounded, including the chief centurion, Publius Sextius Baculus, the bravest of the brave, who was so exhausted by a number of severe wounds that he could no longer keep his feet; the men had lost all dash, and some in the rear ranks had abandoned their posts and were slinking away from the field and getting out of range;

while the enemy were coming up in front in an unbroken stream from below, and closing in on both flanks: in short, the situation was critical and there was no reserve, available. Seeing all this, Caesar, who had come up without a shield, took one from a soldier in the rear rank, stepped forward into the front rank, and, addressing the centurions by name, encouraged the men and told them to advance, opening their ranks so that they might be able to use their swords more readily. His coming inspired them with hope and gave them new heart; and as everyone, even in his most extreme peril, was anxious to do his utmost under the eyes of his general, the enemy's onset was in some measure checked.

Noticing that the 7th legion, which stood close by, was likewise hard pressed by the enemy, Caesar told the tribunes to make the legions gradually approach one another, face the enemy on all sides, and advance. This was done; and, as the men now gave each other mutual support and were not afraid of being taken in rear, they began to offer a more confident resistance and to fight with more resolution. Meanwhile the men of the two legions which had brought up the rear and guarded the baggage, having received news of the action, had quickened their pace and were descried on the brow of the hill by the enemy; and Titus Labienus, who had captured the enemy's camp and observed from the high ground what was going on in ours, sent the 10th legion to the assistance of our men. Realizing from the flight of the cavalry and servants how-matters stood, and seeing that camp, legions, and general were in great peril, they put forth their utmost speed.

Their arrival wrought such a complete change that, on our side, even men who had lain down severely wounded learned on their shields and renewed the fight: the servants, noticing the enemy's alarm, rushed upon them, unarmed against armed; while the cavalry, anxious to wipe out the disgrace of their flight by gallant deeds, out vied the legionaries at every point. But the enemy, even in their despair, displayed such heroic courage that, when their foremost ranks had fallen, the next mounted upon their prostrate comrades and fought standing on their bodies; and when they too were struck down and the corpses littered in a heap, the survivors hurled as from a mound their missiles against our men, and picked up and flung back their javelins. We are not to think, then, that it was in vain that these gallant men dared to cross a broad river, to climb high banks, and to assail a formidable position. These things, in themselves most difficult, had been made easy by their heroism.

The battle was over and the Nervian people, nay their very name, was brought to the verge of extinction. On hearing the news, the old people, who, as we have said, had taken refuge, along with the women and children, in tidal creeks and in swamps, believing that there was nothing to stop the victors and no security for the vanquished, sent envoys to Caesar with the consent of all the survivors, and surrendered; and, recounting the calamity which had befallen their country, they affirmed that their council had been reduced from six hundred to three, and the number of men capable of bearing arms from sixty thousand to a bare five hundred. Caesar, wishing to establish his character for mercy towards unfortunate suppliants, was careful to shield them from harm, authorized them to retain possession of their territories and strongholds, and commanded their neighbors to abstain and to make their dependents abstain from maltreating or molesting them.

The Aduatuci, whose movements we have already described, were coming with all their refuge in forces to the assistance of the Nervii, when, on the announcement of the battle, they turned without halting and went home. Abandoning all their other strongholds and fortified posts, they removed all their belongings into one fortress of extraordinary natural strength. All round, it presented a line of high rocks and steep declivities, which at one point left a gently sloping approach, not more than two hundred feet wide. This place the garrison had fortified with a double wall of great height, upon which, as a further protection, they were laying stones of great weight and sharp-pointed beams. The Aduatuci were descended from the Cimbri and Teutoni, who, on their march for our Province and Italy, left the stock and baggage which they were unable to drive or carry with them, on this side of the Rhine, with some of their number to look after them and six thousand men to protect them. After the fate of their countrymen this band was for many years harassed by the neighboring peoples, sometimes attacking, at other times repelling attack: at length they made peace, and with the consent of all the other tribes selected this district as their abode.

Immediately after the arrival of our army, the Aduatuci made a series of sorties from the town and engaged in skirmishes with our troops; afterwards, however, finding themselves shut in by a rampart twelve feet high and three miles in extent, with numerous redoubts, they kept inside the stronghold. A line of sheds was formed and a terrace constructed; and seeing a tower in process of erection some way off, they at first jeered and made abusive remarks from the wall at the idea of such a huge machine being erected at such a distance. Did those pygmy Romans, with their feeble hands and puny muscles (the Gauls, as a rule, despise our short stature, contrasting it with their own great height), believe themselves able to mount such a ponderous tower on the wall?

When, however, they saw it in motion and actually approaching the walls, the strange and unwanted spectacle alarmed them, and they sent envoys to Caesar to sue for peace. The envoys, saying that Roman warriors were evidently not left unaided by the gods, since they could propel such towering engines at such a rate, declared themselves ready to surrender unreservedly. One thing only they would beg him not to do—if haply in his mercy and forbearance, of which they heard from other peoples, he had decided to spare the Aduatuci — not to deprive them of their arms. Almost all their neighbors were their bitter enemies and jealous of their prowess, and if they surrendered their arms, they could not defend themselves against them. If they were reduced to the alternative, it would be better for them to suffer any fate at the hands of the Romans rather than to be tortured to death by men among whom they were accustomed to hold sway.

To this appeal Caesar replied that he would spare the tribe, not because they deserved mercy, but because it was his wont to be merciful, provided they surrendered before the ram touched the wall; but the question of surrender could not be entertained unless they gave up their arms. He would act as he had acted in the case of the Nervii, and order their neighbors not to molest those who had surrendered to the Roman People. The envoys, after reporting his decision to their principals, professed themselves ready to obey his commands. A great quantity of arms was pitched down from the wall into the trench in front of the town, the heap almost reaching the top of the wall and of the terrace; and yet, as was afterwards discovered, about one-third was concealed and kept in the town. The gates were then thrown open; and on the same day the garrison entered upon the enjoyment of peace.

Towards evening Caesar ordered the gates to be shut and the soldiers to leave the town, for fear the inhabitants should suffer any injury at their hands in the night. They had evidently prearranged a plan. Believing that, after the capitulation, our troops would withdraw their piquets, or at any rate be less vigilant in maintaining them, and taking the arms which they had kept back and concealed, as well as shields made of bark or wattle-work, which, being pressed for time, they had hastily covered with skins, they made a sudden sortie in the third watch with their whole force at the point where the slope leading up to our entrenchments appeared easiest. The alarm was promptly given, in obedience to orders which Caesar had issued in anticipation, by fire-signals; and troops hurried to the point from the nearest redoubts. The enemy's whole hope of safety depended upon courage alone; and they fought with the fierce energy that was to be expected from brave men, fighting on a forlorn hope, on unfavorable ground, against opponents who were hurling their missiles from rampart and towers. About four thousand were killed, and the rest driven back into the town. Next day, as there was no longer any resistance, the gates were burst open; the soldiers were sent in; and Caesar sold by auction, in one lot, all the booty of war found in the town. The purchasers reported the number of individuals as fifty-three thousand.

At the same time Caesar was informed by Publius Crassus, whom he had sent with a single legion to the territories of the Veneti, Osismi, Coriosolites, Esuvii, Aulerci, and Redones — maritime tribes whose country reaches the Ocean—that all of them had been brought completely under the dominion of the Roman People.

These operations resulted in the pacification of the whole of Gaul; and the natives were so impressed by the story of the campaign which reached them, that the peoples who dwelt beyond the Rhine sent envoys to Caesar, promising to give hostages and fulfil his commands. Being anxious to get to Italy and Illyricum without delay, he ordered the envoys to return to him at the commencement of the following summer. Quartering his legions for the winter in the territories of the Carnutes, Andes, Turoni, and other tribes which were near the theatre of the recent campaign, he started for Italy. On the receipt of his dispatches, a thanksgiving service of fifteen days was appointed to celebrate his achievements—an honor which had not hitherto fallen to the lot of anyone.

BOOK III

Galba's campaign in the Valais –
Campaigns against the maritime tribes and the Aquitani

When Caesar was starting for Italy, he sent Servius Galba with the 12th legion and a detachment of cavalry to the country belonging to the Nantuates, Veragri, and Seduni, which extends from the frontier of the Allobroges, the Lake of Geneva, and the Rhone to the crest of the Alps, being anxious to open up the route over the Alps, by which traders usually travelled at great risk and with the obligation of paying heavy tolls. Galba was authorized to quarter his legion in the district for the winter, if he thought it necessary. After he had gained several victories and taken a number of forts belonging to the tribesmen, they sent envoys to him from all parts, gave hostages, and made peace; whereupon he determined to quarter two cohorts in the country of the Nantuates, and to winter with the remaining cohorts of the legion in a village, belonging to the Veragri, called Octodurus. The village, which is situated in a valley, and adjoined by a plain of moderate extent, is walled in on every side by lofty mountains. It was divided by a stream into two parts, one of which he allowed the Gauls to occupy, while he reserved the vacant part for the winter quarters of the cohorts, and fortified the position with a rampart and trench.

Several days had been spent in camp, and Galba had ordered grain to be brought in, when suddenly he was informed by his patrols that during the night the Gauls had all quitted the part of the village which he had allotted to them, and that the overhanging mountains were occupied by a numerous host of Seduni and Veragri. Various reasons had led the Gauls to form the sudden resolution of renewing hostilities and overpowering the legion. First, the legion was numerically so weak that they despised it; it had not been at its full strength originally, and two cohorts, as well as numerous individuals who had been sent out to get supplies, had been withdrawn. Again, as the Romans had the worst of the ground, while they would themselves hurl their missiles, charging down into the valley from the hills, they were confident that their first onslaught would be irresistible. Besides, they resented their children being taken from them as hostages; and they were convinced that the Romans were trying to occupy the commanding points of the Alps, and to annex the district to the neighboring Province, not merely in order to open up communication, but to secure permanent possession.

Octodurus was between Martigny-la-Ville and the more southerly Martigny-Bourg, on the left bank of the Rhone, near the point where it bends northward towards the Lake of Geneva. Galba's camp was on the left bank of the Dranse, a tributary of the Rhone, which then flowed in a different channel down the middle of the valley. The work of entrenching the camp was not yet quite completed, and corn and other supplies war had not been provided in sufficient quantity, for Galba had concluded that, as the enemy had submitted and he had received their hostages, there was no reason to fear hostilities: accordingly, on receiving the news, he promptly called a council of war, and invited opinions. A great peril had befallen suddenly and unexpectedly, already, indeed, almost all the heights were seen to be swarming with armed men; the roads were blocked, and therefore it was impossible for relief to arrive or for supplies to be brought up; and safety was deemed all but hopeless: some, therefore, expressed the opinion that they ought to abandon the baggage, make a sortie, and try to reach a place of safety by the same route by which they had come. The majority, however, decided to reserve this plan to the last, and meanwhile to defend the camp and await developments. After a short interval, which barely gave time for making the dispositions and carrying out the arrangements which had been resolved upon, the enemy rushed down at a given signal from every side, and hurled stones and javelins on to the rampart. At first, while our men were still fresh, they resisted stoutly, not a missile which they threw from their commanding position missing its mark; and when any part of the camp that was inadequately manned appeared to be hard pressed, men hurried to the rescue: but what told against them was that when the enemy were exhausted by prolonged fighting they went out of action, and fresh men took their places, while our men, owing to their slender numbers, could not follow their example; and not only was it impossible for a man to go out of action when he was tired, but even if wounded he could not leave his post and recover himself.

For more than six hours the fighting had been incessant: not only the strength of our men, but even their missiles were failing; the enemy were pressing on with increased energy, and, as our men grew feebler, they began to fill up the trenches and demolish the rampart. In this extremity Publius Sextius Baculus, the chief centurion, who, as we have said, had received several severe wounds in the battle with the Nervii, ran to Galba, accompanied by Gains Volusenus, a tribune of great judgement and courage, and pointed out that the only chance of safety was to try a forlorn hope and make a sortie. Galba therefore summoned the centurions, and quickly made the men understand that they were to leave off fighting for a little, only parrying the enemy's missiles, rest after their exertions, and afterwards, when the signal was given, charge out of camp and trust for safety to sheer courage.

The order was carried out. Suddenly they charged out of all the gates, and never gave the enemy a chance of divining their intention or of closing their ranks. Fortune had changed sides. The assailants, who had actually hoped to take the camp, were surrounded and slain. More than a third of the entire native force that had assailed the camp, which was known to number over thirty thousand men, were killed; the rest were sent flying in panic; and the Romans would not suffer them to rally even on the heights. Having thus routed the entire hostile force and taken their arms, they returned to their entrenchments.

After fighting this battle, Galba had no wish to tempt fortune any more: he reflected that the circumstances with which he had had to contend were at variance with the purpose for which he had taken up his quarters; and the scarcity of corn and other supplies caused him great anxiety. Next day, therefore, he fired all the buildings in the village and hastened to return to the Province; and, as no enemy attempted to stop him or opposed his march, he brought the legion back safely into the country of the Nantuates, and thence into that of the Allobroges, where he passed the winter. After these operations everything led Caesar to believe that Gaul was tranquillized, for the revolted. Belgae were overpowered, the Germans driven out, and the Seduni defeated in the Alps: accordingly he had started, at the beginning of winter, for Illyricum, being anxious to visit the tribes there as well as those of Gaul, and to make himself acquainted with their country, when suddenly war broke out in Gaul, for the following reason.

The younger Publius Crassus, who was wintering with the 7th legion among the Andes, near the Ocean, finding that corn was scarce in the district, sent a number of auxiliary officers and tribunes to the neighboring tribes to arrange for a supply. Amongst others, Titus Terrasidius was sent to the Esuvii, Marcus Trebius Gallus to the Coriosolites.

The last named tribe is by far the most influential of all the maritime peoples in that part of the country. They possess numerous ships, in which they regularly sail to Britain; they excel in knowledge of navigation and in seamanship; and, the sea being very stormy and open, with only a few scattered harbors, which they keep under their control, they compel almost all who sail those waters to pay toll. They took the initiative by detaining Silius and Velanius, believing that they would be able to use them to get back the hostages whom they had given to Crassus. Their neighbors, influenced by their example, and making up their minds, like true Gauls, suddenly and without consideration, detained Trebius and Terrasidius for the same reason;

hurriedly dispatched envoys, and, through the medium of their leaders, pledged themselves to do nothing without official sanction, and to stand by one another in victory or defeat; and called upon the other tribes to resolve to hold fast to the liberty which they had received from their forefathers, and not to submit to the yoke of the Romans. They speedily gained over all the maritime tribes, and jointly sent an embassy to Publius Crassus, calling upon him, if he wished to recover his officers, to restore their hostages. When Caesar was informed of these events, he was a long way off, and accordingly gave orders that ships of war should be built, before his return, on the Loire, which flows into their ocean.

Oarsmen were raised from the Province, and seamen and pilots assembled. These orders were promptly executed; and, as soon as the season permitted, he [Caesar] hastened to join the army. On hearing of his approach, the Veneti, and also the other tribes, being aware that they had committed a heinous offence in detaining and imprisoning envoys, whose office had always, among all peoples, been held sacred and inviolable, proceeded to make preparations for war — and especially to provide for the equipment of their ships—on a scale commensurate with the magnitude of the danger; and they worked with a hopefulness which was increased by their faith in the natural strength of their country. They knew that the roads were interrupted by estuaries, and that navigation was rendered difficult by the want of topographical information and the scarcity of harbors; they were confident that our armies would not be able to remain long in their country, for want of grain; and, even if all their calculations were upset, they had command of the sea, while the Romans were ill supplied with ships and had no knowledge of the theatre of the approaching war, — the shoals, harbors, and islands; finally, they saw that navigation in a land-locked sea and in the open, boundless ocean were very different things. After forming their plans, they fortified their strongholds, stored them with grain from the country districts, and assembled as many ships as possible in Venetia, where it was known that Caesar would open the campaign. They secured the alliance of the Osismi, Namnetes, Ambiliati and Morini.

The difficulties above mentioned which beset the campaign were serious but nevertheless Caesar had many urgent motives for undertaking it - the violation of international law in detaining Roman knights; the fact that the tribes after submission had renewed hostilities, and revolted although they had given hostages; the wide extension of the conspiracy; and, above all, the danger that, if this district were left unpunished, the other peoples would fancy that they might offend in the same way. Knowing, therefore, that the Gauls were almost all politically restless, and that their warlike passions were easily and swiftly roused, and moreover that all men are naturally fond of freedom and hate to be in subjection, he thought it best, before more tribes had time to join the movement, to break up his army and distribute it over a wider area.

Accordingly he sent Titus Labienus with a body of cavalry into the country of the Treveri, near the Rhine, with orders to visit the Aquitanians, and the other Belgic peoples and keep them obedient; and in case the Germans, whose assistance was said to have been solicited by the Belgae, attempted to force a passage in boats of his fleet across the river, to stop them. Publius Crassus was directed to march with twelve legionary cohorts and a strong body of cavalry for Aquitania, in order to prevent the dispatch of reinforcements to Gaul from the peoples of that country and the junction of two powerful races. Quintus Titurius Sabinus, one of the generals, was sent with three legions into the country of the Venelli, Coriosolites, and Lexovii, to keep that section of the rebels isolated. The younger Decimus Brutus was placed in command of the fleet and of the Gallic ships which Caesar had ordered to assemble from the ports of the Pictones and Santoni and from the other settled districts, with orders to sail, as soon as possible, for the country of the Veneti. Caesar marched thither in person with the land forces.

The strongholds were generally situated on the ends of spits or headlands that it was impossible to approach them on foot, when the tide came rushing in from the open sea (which regularly happens every twelve hours), or to sail up to them, because at the ebb the ships would have been injured in the shallow water. Both of these causes interfered with the siege of the strongholds. The besiegers kept out the sea by building dykes, and by this means got on a level with the walls of the town; but when the besieged, overmatched by the magnitude of the works, began to lose confidence, they brought up a large number of ships, of which they had an unlimited supply, removed all their property, and withdrew to the nearest strongholds, where they again defended themselves by the same advantages of position. These tactics they found it easy to keep up during a great part of the summer, because our ships were detained by stormy weather, and navigation was very difficult in a vast open sea, where the tides were strong and harbors few and far between, indeed practically non-existent.

Their own ships were built and fitted out in the following way. They were a good deal more flat-bottomed than ours, to adapt them to the conditions of shallow water and ebbing tides. Bows and sterns alike were very lofty, being thus enabled to resist heavy seas and severe gales. The hulls were built throughout of oak, in order to stand any amount of violence and rough usage. The cross-timbers, consisting of beams a foot thick, were riveted with iron bolts as thick as a man's thumb. The anchors were secured with iron chains instead of ropes. Hides or leather dressed fine were used instead of sails, either because flax was scarce and the natives did not know how to manufacture it, or, more probably, because they thought it difficult to make head against the violent storms and squalls of the Ocean, and to manage vessels of such burden with ordinary sails. When these ships encountered our fleet, the latter had the advantage only in speed and in being propelled by oars; in other respects the former, from their more suitable construction, were better adapted to the conditions of the coast and the force of the storms. They were so solidly built that our ships could not injure them by ramming; owing to their height, it was not easy to throw javelins onto them; and for the same reason it was difficult to seize them with grappling irons. Moreover, when it began to blow hard and they were running before the wind, they could weather the storm more easily; they could lie up more safely in shallow water; and when they were left aground by the ebb, they had nothing to fear from a stony bottom and sharp rocks; whereas our ships were in great danger from all these contingencies. After taking several strongholds, Caesar saw that all his labour was being expended in vain, and that, by merely capturing their forts, he could neither prevent the enemy from escaping nor cripple them. He decided, therefore, that it would be best to wait for his fleet. As soon as it arrived and was sighted by the enemy, their ships, numbering about two hundred and twenty, ready for sea and fully equipped, stood out of harbor and ranged opposite ours. Brutus, who commanded the fleet, and the tribunes and centurions, each of whom had been entrusted with a single ship, did not quite know what to do, or what tactics to adopt. They had ascertained that it was impossible to injure the enemy's ships by ramming. The turrets were run up; but even then they were overtopped by the lofty sterns, so that, from the lower position, it was impossible to throw javelins with effect, while the missiles thrown by the Gauls fell with increased momentum.

Our men, however, had a very effective contrivance ready, namely, hooks, sharpened at the ends and fixed to long poles, shaped somewhat like grappling-hooks. By means of these the halyards were seized and pulled taut: the galley rowed hard; and the ropes snapped. When they were cut, the yards of course fell down; and as the efficiency of the Gallic ships depended altogether upon their sails and rigging, when they were gone the ships were no longer of any use. Thenceforward the struggle turned upon sheer courage, in which our soldiers easily had the advantage, especially as the fighting went on under the eyes of Caesar and the whole army, so that no act of courage at all remarkable could escape notice; for all the cliffs and high ground which commanded a near view over the sea were occupied by the army.

When, as we have said, the yards tumbled down, the Roman ships, two or three at a time, closed round one of the enemy's; and the legionaries clambered aboard with the utmost vigor. Several ships had been captured, when the natives, seeing what was happening and realizing that there was no help for it, hastened to save themselves by flight. And now, just as the ships had been put before the wind, there was suddenly a dead calm, and they could not stir. This was just what was wanted to make the victory complete. Our men gave chase and captured the ships one after another, with the result that, after a battle lasting from about the fourth hour till sunset, only a very few of the whole armada managed, when night stopped the pursuit, to make the land.

This battle brought the war with the Veneti and all the coast tribes to an end; for all the fighting men, and indeed all the seniors of any standing or whose counsels had any weight, had taken part in it: they had brought every one of their ships into action; and now that they were lost, the survivors had no place to escape to and no means of defending their strongholds. They surrendered, therefore, to Caesar unreservedly. He determined to inflict upon them a signal punishment, in order to make the natives respect the rights of ambassadors more carefully in future. Accordingly he put to death the entire council, and sold the rest of the population into slavery.

While these events were passing in the country of the Veneti, Quintus Titurius Sabinus made his way with the troops assigned to him by Caesar into the country of the Venelli. Their leader was Viridovix, who was also commander-in-chief of all the insurgent tribes, and had raised from them an army and large irregular levies. Within the few days that followed Sabinus's arrival, the Aulerci, Eburovices and the Lexovii massacred their senators because they refused to sanction the war, shut their gates, and joined Viridovix; and a host of desperadoes and brigands had also assembled from all parts of Gaul, to whom the hope of plunder and love of fighting were more attractive than farming and regular work. Sabinus, who occupied a position in all respects excellent, remained obstinately in camp; while Viridovix, who had encamped opposite him, two miles off, led out his troops every day and offered battle. The result was that Sabinus not only incurred the contempt of the enemy, but was actually the object of some abuse from his own troops; and he let the enemy become so convinced of his timidity that they presently ventured to approach close to the rampart. His motive was that he felt bound, as a subordinate, especially in the absence of his chief, to avoid engaging such a numerous enemy unless he had the best of the ground or some favourable opportunity presented itself.

Now that they were convinced of his timidity, he selected from his auxiliaries a quick-witted Gaul, the very man for his purpose, induced him by liberal rewards and promises to go over to the enemy, and explained his object. The man came to them in the guise of a deserter; described the terror of the Romans; and explained that Caesar himself was hard pressed by the Veneti, and that Sabinus would march his army stealthily out of camp not later than the following night and go to his assistance. On hearing this, they all cried that the chance of striking a decisive blow was not to be lost: they must attack the camp. Many circumstances combined to impel them to this decision,—the recent inaction of Sabinus, the assurances of the deserter, want of supplies (for which they had made scant provision), the hope that the Veneti would succeed in their campaign, and lastly, the fact that what men desire they are generally prone to believe. Influenced by these motives, they would not suffer Viridovix and the other leaders to leave the assembly until they had agreed to let them arm and make a dash for the camp. When they were allowed to have their way they were as exultant as if victory were certain, and, collecting brushwood and faggots to fill up the Roman trenches, they advanced against the camp.

The camp stood on rising ground, which sloped gently from its base for about a mile. The Gauls hurried up at a great pace, in order to give the Romans the least possible time for falling into line and arming, and arrived breathless. Sabinus harangued his men, and gave the signal which they were eagerly awaiting. As the enemy were hampered by their loads, he ordered a sudden sortie from two of the gates. Thanks to the favourable position, the courage of the legionaries and the experience which they had gained in previous combats, and their own want of skill and exhaustion, the enemy instantly turned tail without standing a single charge from our men. They were in no condition to escape, and our troops, who were fresh for pursuit, killed a great number of them. The rest were hunted down by the cavalry, who allowed few to get away. Thus Sabinus heard of the sea-fight and Caesar of Sabinus's victory at the same time; and all the tribes immediately submitted to Titurius. For, while the Gallic temperament is impetuous and warlike, their character is irresolute and has little power of bearing up against disaster.

About the same time Crassus arrived in Aquitania, which, as the narrative has shown, may be regarded, in area and population, as one-third of Gaul. Knowing that he had to fight in a country where, a few years before, a Roman general, Lucius Valerius Praeconinus, had been killed and his army defeated, and from which a proconsul, Lucius Manlius, had retreated in disorder with the loss of his baggage, he saw that he would have to exercise no ordinary care. Accordingly he provided for a supply of grain, raised auxiliaries and cavalry, and also called out individually a large number of excellent soldiers from Tolosa, Carcaso, and Narbo—states in the Province, adjacent to Aquitania — and marched his army into the country of the Sotiates. On becoming aware of his approach, they raised a large force, including cavalry, and attacked our column on its march. The battle began with a combat of horse. Their cavalry were repulsed and ours were pursuing them, when suddenly they unmasked their infantry, which they had stationed in ambush in a valley. The latter fell upon our disordered troops and renewed the action.

The fighting was prolonged and fierce; for the Sotiates relied upon their past victories and felt that the fate of all Aquitania depended upon their courage; while our men were eager that the world should see what they could achieve under their youthful leader, without the chief and the other legions. At length the enemy, having suffered heavy loss, turned and fled. Many of them were slain; and Crassus, advancing to the chief town of the Sotiates, at once proceeded to lay siege to it. As the garrison offered a stout resistance, he brought up sheds and towers. The garrison first attempted a sortie, then drove galleries in the direction of the terrace and sheds (the Aquitanians are very skilled in operations of this kind, as mining works exist in many parts of their country); but finding that, owing to the vigilance of our troops, they could affect nothing by these devices, they sent envoys to Crassus, asking him to accept their surrender. Their request was granted; and, in obedience to his command, they laid down their arms. But all was not over. Our men were all intently watching what was going on, when Adiatunnus, who was in command, attempted a sortie from another part of the town with six hundred devoted followers, whom the natives call *soldurity* —men who, while life lasts, share all good things with the friends to whom they have attached themselves, on the understanding that, if any violence befall them, they are either to share their fate or to die by their own hands; and within the memory of man no one has ever been known to shrink from death when his friend and leader was slain. With these men Adiatunnus attempted a sortie; but when the roar of battle arose from that part of the entrenchment, the soldiers ran to arms, and, after hard fighting, Adiatunnus was driven back into the town. Notwithstanding, he prevailed upon Crassus to allow him to surrender on the original terms.

On receiving the arms and hostages, Crassus started for the country of the Vocates tribes and Tarusates. And now, learning that a fortified town of great natural strength had been captured a few days after the arrival of the besiegers, the natives were thoroughly alarmed and began to send envoys in all directions, to swear mutual fidelity, to exchange hostages, and to raise troops. Envoys were also sent to the tribes of Higher Spain, near Aquitania, with a request for reinforcements and leaders, whose arrival enabled them to undertake the campaign with great prestige and to put a large number of men in the field. The leaders chosen had served from first to last with Quintus Sertorius, and were believed to possess great military skill. Adopting Roman methods, they proceeded to select positions, to entrench their camp, and to cut off our convoys. Crassus, reflecting that his own force was too small to be readily divided, that the enemy, while scouring the country and blocking the roads, were able to leave a sufficient force to protect their camp, which made it difficult to bring up corn and other supplies, and that their numbers were daily increasing, thought it best to fight a decisive battle without delay. He referred the question to a council of war, and, finding that everyone agreed with him, determined to fight on the morrow.

At daybreak he moved out the whole force, formed them in two lines with the auxiliaries in the center, and awaited the development of the enemy's plans. Although, relying on their numbers, their established military reputation, and the weakness of our force, they considered it safe to fight, they nevertheless thought it safer to gain a bloodless victory by blocking the roads and cutting off our supplies; while, in case the Romans began to retreat from want of food, their idea was to attack them on the march, when their movements were impeded and they had their packs to carry and were dispirited. The plan was approved by their leaders; and accordingly when the Roman army moved out they remained shut up in camp. Crassus divined their intention. Their inaction, which produced the belief that they were cowed, had stimulated the ardor of our troops for battle, and all were overheard saying that the camp ought to be attacked without further delay; so Crassus, haranguing his men, who were all in great heart, advanced rapidly against the enemy's camp.

Some filled up the trenches; others drove the defenders from the rampart and fortifications with volleys of missiles; and the auxiliaries, in whose soldierly qualities Crassus had not much faith, kept the combatants supplied with stones and other missiles, brought up sods for filling the trench, and thus made a decent show of fighting. The enemy, too, fought steadily and with no lack of courage; and the missiles which they threw from their commanding position did good execution. Meanwhile some troopers rode round the enemy's camp and reported to Crassus that on the side of the rear gate it was not entrenched so carefully as elsewhere and offered easy entrance.

Crassus urged his cavalry officers to stimulate their men by liberal rewards and promises, and explained his object. In obedience to orders, they marched out the cohorts which had been left to protect the camp and had had nothing to tire them; made a wide detour, to avoid being observed from the enemy's camp; and, while everybody was intent upon the action and noticed nothing else, rapidly gained the part of the entrenchments which we have mentioned, demolished them, and made good their footing in the camp before the enemy could clearly see them or make out what was going on.

And now, when our troops heard the shouting from that part of the camp, their strength returned, as generally happens when soldiers feel confident of victory, and they fought with redoubled energy.

Finding themselves surrounded, the enemy in utter despair hastened to throw themselves over the entrenchments and ran for their lives. The cavalry hunted them over the broad open plains; out of fifty thousand who were known to have come from Aquitania and the land of the Cantabri, barely a fourth escaped them; and late at night they returned to camp.

On hearing the result of the battle, the bulk of the population of Aquitania, including the Tarbelli, Bigerriones, Ptianii, Vocates, Tarusates, Elusates, Gates, Ausci, Garumni, Sibusates, and Cocosates, submitted to Crassus and voluntarily sent hostages.

About the same time Caesar led his army against the Morini and the Menapii, in the belief that the campaign could be soon finished. The summer was nearly over; but, while all the rest of Gaul was tranquillized, they remained in arms, and had never sent envoys to him to sue for peace. Their tactics were quite different from those of the other Gauls. Being aware that the strongest tribes which had fought in the open field had been completely defeated, they took refuge, with all their belongings, in their continuous forests and marshes. On reaching the outskirts of the forests, Caesar proceeded to entrench his camp. No enemy had so far appeared, and the men were working in scattered groups, when suddenly the enemy rushed out of the forest from all sides and attacked them. The men quickly seized their weapons and drove them back into the forest with considerable loss; but, pursuing them too far over very difficult ground, lost a few of their own number.

Caesar now proceeded to clear the forest, and continued doing so day after day. To prevent the soldiers from being attacked in flank while they were unarmed and off their guard, he regularly laid the timber as it was felled in the direction of the enemy, and piled it as a barricade on both flanks. A large space was cleared with incredible speed in a few days, by which time the enemy's cattle and the rear portion of their baggage were in our hands, while they were making for the denser parts of the forest: but such stormy weather followed that the work had to be discontinued; and, owing to continuous rains, it was impossible to keep the soldiers longer under tents. Accordingly, after ravaging but is forced all the enemy's fields and burning their hamlets and homesteads, Caesar withdrew his troops and quartered them for the winter in the territories of the Aulerci, the Lexovii, and the other tribes which had recently been in arms.

BOOK IV

The fate of the Usipetes and Tencteri—
Caesar's first invasion of Britain

In the following winter—the year in which Cn. Pompey and M. Crassus were consuls—a German tribe, the Usipetes, accompanied by the Tencteri, crossed the Rhine in large numbers, not far from the point where it enters the sea. Their motive was that for several years they had been subject to harassing attacks from the Suevi, and prevented from tilling the land. The Suevi are by far the most numerous and warlike of all the German peoples. They are said to comprise a hundred clans, each of which annually sends a thousand armed men on a military expedition beyond the frontier. The rest of the population remain at home, and support the expeditionary force as well as themselves. Next year they take up arms in their turn, and the others remain at home. Thus agriculture goes on uninterruptedly along with theoretical and practical training in war. Private property in land, however, does not exist; and no one is allowed to remain for farming in one spot longer than a year. Not much corn, indeed, is consumed; the people live principally on milk and flesh-meat, and spend much time in hunting. This, combined with the nature of their food, their constant exercise and freedom from restraint (for they have never, from childhood, been made to obey or subjected to discipline, and never do anything against their inclination), fosters their bodily vigor and produces a race of gigantic stature. Moreover, they have trained themselves to wear no clothing, even in the coldest districts, except skins, which leave a large part of the body bare, and to bathe in the rivers.

Traders are allowed to enter their country, not because they want to import anything but that they may find purchasers for their booty. Even horses, of which the Gauls are extremely fond, and to procure which they go to great expense, are not imported by the Germans. The native horses are undersized and ugly, but by constant exercise they develop in them extraordinary powers of endurance. In cavalry combats they often dismount and fight on foot, training their horses to stand still, and quickly remounting when necessary. According to their notions, nothing is more shameful or unmanly than the use of saddles; and so, however small their numbers, they are ready to encounter any number of cavalry who use them. They will not allow wine to be imported at all, considering that its use enfeebles a man's power of endurance and makes him effeminate.

The communities as such pride themselves on keeping the land round their own borders uninhabited as far as possible, regarding it as a proof that many tribes are unable to cope with them. Thus it is said that on one side of the Suevan territory there is an uninhabited tract extending about six hundred miles. On the opposite side, their neighbors are the Ubii, who were once a considerable, and, according to German standards, flourishing tribe. They are in fact rather more civilized than the rest of the nation; for they are near the Rhine, their country is much frequented by traders, and, from propinquity, they have become familiarized with Gallic customs. The Suevi, after many campaigns and frequent attempts, had found them too numerous and powerful to be dispossessed; but they made them tributary and reduced them to comparative insignificance and weakness. The Usipetes and Tencteri, mentioned above, were in the same position. For several years they withstood the pressure of the Suevi; but at length they were dispossessed, and, after wandering three years through many parts of Germany, came to the Rhine. The Menapii inhabited that region, and owned lands, homesteads, and villages on both banks of the river; but alarmed by the incursion of this huge host, they abandoned their dwellings on the further bank, established outposts on this side of the Rhine, and determined to prevent the Germans from crossing. The latter tried every expedient; but being unable to force a passage from want of boats or to get across unobserved because of the Menapian patrols, pretended to return to the district where they had settled, marched on for three days, and then turned back again. Their cavalry made the whole journey in a single night, and swooped down upon the Menapii, who, knowing nothing of their movements, were off their guard, and, having been informed by their patrols that they had gone off, had fearlessly recrossed the Rhine and returned to their villages. The Germans slaughtered them; seized their boats; crossed the river before the Menapii on this side of the Rhine could tell what they were about; took possession of all their buildings; and for the rest of the winter lived on their stores.

The unstable character of the Gauls caused Caesar anxiety, for they do not abide by their decisions, and are generally prone to revolution: accordingly, when he learned the facts, he thought it best not to rely upon them at all. It is a custom of theirs to detain travelers, even against their will, and question them individually about what they have heard or ascertained on this or that topic; and in the towns the people cluster round traders and make them, say where they come from and tell them the news. Influenced by these reports, even when they are merely hearsay, they often embark upon the most momentous enterprises; and, as they trust blindly to vague gossip, and their informants generally tell lies and frame their answers to please them, they naturally repent of their plans as soon as they are formed.

Caesar was aware of this custom, and, to avoid having a serious war on his hands, he started to rejoin his army earlier than usual. On his arrival he found that his forebodings were justified: embassies had been sent by more than one tribe to the Germans, inviting them to quit the neighborhood of the Rhine, and promising to supply all their requirements. Allured by this prospect, they were now wandering further afield and had reached the territories of the Eburones and Condrusi,—both dependents of the Treveri. Caesar summoned the Gallic notables, and, thinking it well to dissemble what he knew, addressed them in soothing and reassuring terms, directed them to furnish cavalry, and announced his intention of taking the field against the Germans.

After arranging for a supply of grain and selecting troopers from the several contingents, he began his march towards the districts in which he heard that the Germans were encamped. When he was within a few days' march from them, their envoys arrived, and addressed him as follows:—the Germans were not the aggressors, but, if they were provoked, they would not shrink from a contest with the Roman People; for it was a principle of theirs, handed down by their forefathers, to resist all who attacked them, and not to sue for mercy. Still, this much they would say,—they had come reluctantly, because they had been driven from their country. If the Romans cared for their goodwill, their friendship might be of use to them: let the Romans either assign them lands or suffer them to retain those which they had won by the sword. They acknowledged the superiority of the Suevi alone, for even the immortal gods were no match for them; and there was no other people upon earth whom they could not overcome.

Caesar made a suitable reply. The upshot of his speech was that there could be no friendship between him and the Germans if they remained in Gaul. It was not reasonable for land of the people who could not defend their own territories to take possession of those of others; and besides, there were no unoccupied lands in Gaul which could be made over to any people, least of all to one so numerous, without injustice. Still, they might settle, if they wished, in the country of the Ubii, whose envoys were with him, complaining of the ill-treatment of the Suevi and asking for his aid; and he would order the Ubii to receive them.

The envoys said that they would refer this offer to their principals, and, after it had been considered, would return to Caesar in three days; meanwhile they requested him not to move nearer. Caesar told them that it was impossible for him to make even this concession. He had ascertained that a large detachment of their cavalry had been sent across the Meuse some days before to the country of the Ambivariti, to plunder and forage; and he believed that they were waiting for their return, and that that was their motive for trying to gain time.

The Meuse rises in the Vosges mountains, which are in the territory of the Lingones, receives an affluent called the Waal from the Rhine, thereby forming the island of the Batavi, and not more than eighty miles from that point flows into the Ocean. The Rhine rises in the country of the Lepontii, who inhabit the Alps, and flows swiftly for a long distance through the territories of the Nantuates, Helvetii, Sequani, Mediomatrici, Triboci, and Treveri: as it approaches the sea it branches off into several channels, and forms numerous large islands, many of which are inhabited by fierce rude tribes, some of whom are supposed to live on fish and birds' eggs, and discharges itself by numerous outlets into the ocean.

When Caesar was not more than twelve miles from the enemy, their envoys returned to see him, according to agreement, and meeting him earnestly entreated him to advance no further. As they could not induce him to comply, they begged him to send word to the cavalry, which had gone on in advance of the column, forbidding them to fight, and to let them send envoys to the Ubii; declaring that if their council and chiefs swore to keep faith with them, they would avail themselves of the terms which he offered, and asking him to give them three days to complete the arrangements. Caesar believed that all these stipulations had the same object,— to secure three days' delay for the return of the absent cavalry; still, he said that he would advance four miles and no more that day, to get water; on the morrow as many of them as could come were to assemble at his halting-place, that he might take cognizance of their requests. Meanwhile he sent messengers to tell the cavalry officers, who had gone on in front with their whole force, not to attack the enemy, and, in case they were attacked themselves, to remain on the defensive till he came up with the rest of the army.

Our cavalry, who numbered five thousand, felt no anxiety, as the German envoys had asked for an armistice for that day, and had only just left Caesar. The moment the enemy caught sight of them, although they had not more than eight hundred horse, those who had crossed the Meuse to forage not having yet returned, they charged and speedily threw them into confusion; and when they rallied, the enemy, following their regular practice, sprang to the ground, stabbed the horses in the belly and unhorsed a number of our men, sent the rest flying, and swept them along in such panic that they never drew rein till they came in sight of our column. Seventy-four of our troopers were killed in the affair, including Piso, a gallant Aquitanian of most illustrious family, whose grandfather had been honored by the Senate with the title of Friend, and had held sovereignty in his own tribe. His brother was surrounded by the enemy, but he went to his assistance and rescued him, and though his horse was wounded, and he was thrown, he resisted most gallantly as long as he could: surrounded and covered with wounds, he fell, when his brother, who had by this time got away from the press and was some distance off, saw what had happened, and putting spurs to his horse, rode straight against the enemy and perished.

After this combat, Caesar no longer felt bound to listen to the envoys, or to entertain the proposals of a people who, after asking for peace, instantly had made a treacherous, insidious, and unprovoked attack. On the other hand, he thought that it would be the height of folly to wait till the enemy were reinforced by the return of their cavalry: from his knowledge of the unstable character of the Gauls, he realized that the enemy, by a single victory, had already gained great prestige with them; and he thought it best to give them no time to form their plans. Having come to this decision, he communicated to his quaestor and generals his determination not to lose a day in forcing on a battle, when a most fortunate event occurred. Next day, early in the morning, a numerous deputation of the Germans, comprising all the leading men and all those of mature age, came to the camp, in the same spirit of treachery and deceit, to wait upon him. Their ostensible object was to clear themselves from complicity in the attack which had taken place the day before, contrary to the agreement which they had themselves asked for; at the same time they intended, if possible, to gain an extension of the armistice on some pretext. Caesar was delighted that they had put themselves in his power, and ordered them to be detained: he then marched out of camp at the head of his whole force, ordering the cavalry, whom he believed to be demoralized by the recent combat, to bring up the rear. Forming the army in three lines, he made a rapid march of eight miles, and reached the enemy's camp before the Germans could realize what was going to happen. The rapidity of our advance and the absence of their leaders suddenly and completely unnerved them; there was no time to consider or to arm; and they were too distracted to know whether it was best to throw their strength against the enemy, to defend the camp, or to fly for their lives. Their terror was manifested by cries and hurried movements, and the soldiers, exasperated by the treachery of the previous day, burst into the camp. Those who were quick enough to seize their weapons made a brief stand there against our men, fighting under cover of their wagons and baggage: but the host of women and children (for they had left their country and crossed the Rhine with all their belongings) began to flee in all directions; and Caesar sent his cavalry to hunt them down.

The Germans heard the shrieks behind, and, seeing that their kith and kin were being slaughtered, threw away their weapons, abandoned their standards, and rushed out of the camp. When they reached the confluence of the Moselle and the Rhine great numbers were already killed; and the rest, giving up all hope of escape, plunged into the stream and there perished, overcome by terror, weariness, and the force of the current. Our men had anxiously anticipated an arduous struggle, for the enemy's numbers had amounted to four hundred and thirty thousand; but all to a man returned safe to camp with only a very few wounded. Caesar gave the prisoners whom he had detained in camp the option of going free; but, as they were afraid of being punished and tortured by the Gauls whose lands they had ravaged, they said that they would prefer to remain with him, and he permitted them to do so.

The campaign against the Germans being concluded, Caesar thought it advisable for many reasons to cross the Rhine. The most cogent reason was this:—observing that the Germans were so ready to invade Gaul, he desired to make them feel alarm on their own account, and realize that the army of the Roman People could and would cross the Rhine. There was another consideration. That division of the cavalry of the Usipetes and Tencteri which, as I have already related, had crossed the Meuse to plunder and forage and had taken no part in the action, had re-crossed the Rhine after the rout of their countrymen, taken refuge in the territory of the Sugambri, and joined forces with them. When Caesar sent envoys to the Sugambri, calling upon them to deliver up the fugitives on the ground that they had made war upon him and upon Gaul, they replied that the Rhine was the limit of Roman dominion: if Caesar thought that the Germans had no right to cross over into Gaul without his permission, how could he claim any authority or power beyond the Rhine? The Ubii, on the other hand, who, alone among these peoples, had sent envoys to Caesar, entered into friendly relations with him, and given hostages, earnestly entreated him to help them, as they were hard pressed by the Suevi, or, if he were prevented from doing so by reasons of state, merely to throw his army across the Rhine, which would be sufficient to support them and assure their prospects for the future. The name and fame which his army had gained, even with the most distant German peoples, by defeating Ariovistus and by this recent victory, were so great that they could safely rely on the prestige and friendship of the Roman People. At the same time they promised to provide a large flotilla of boats for the passage of the army.

Caesar was determined to cross the Rhine for the reasons which I have mentioned; but he thought it hardly safe to cross in boats, and considered that to do so would not be consistent with his own dignity or that of the Roman People. Therefore, although the construction of a bridge presented great difficulties on account of the breadth, swiftness, and depth of the stream, he nevertheless thought it best to make the attempt, or else not to cross at all. The principle upon which he designed the bridge was as follows. He took a couple of piles a foot and a half thick, had them sharpened to a point from a little above the lower end and adapted in length to the varying depth of the river, and fastened them together at an interval of two feet. These piles he caused to be lowered into the river by means of floats, fixed, and driven home with pile-drivers, not vertically, like ordinary piles, but leaning forward in the same plane, so that they followed the direction of the current; then he had another couple of piles, similarly joined together, planted opposite them on the lower side, at a distance of forty feet, against the force and rush of the current. Beams two feet wide, fitting into the interval between the piles of each couple, were laid across; and the two couples were kept apart by a pair of braces on either side at the extremity. The couples being thus kept apart, and on the other hand held firmly in place, the strength of the structure was so great and its principle so ordered that, the greater the force of the current, the more closely were the piles locked together. The series of piles and transverse beams was connected by timbers laid in the direction of the bridge, which were floored with poles and fascines. Finally, notwithstanding the existing strength of the structure, piles were also driven in diagonally on the down-stream side, which were connected with the entire structure and planted below like a buttress, so as to break the force of the stream. Other piles were likewise planted a little above the bridge, so that in case the natives floated down trunks of trees or barges to demolish the structure, their force might be weakened by these bulwarks, and they might not injure the bridge.

Within ten days after the collection of the timber began, the whole work was finished, and the army crossed over. Caesar left a strong force at both ends of the bridge, and marched rapidly for the country of the Sugambri. Meanwhile envoys came in from several tribes; and Caesar replied graciously to their prayer for peace and friendship and directed them to bring him hostages. The Sugambri, on the contrary, from the moment when the construction of the bridge began, acting on the advice of the refugees from the Tencteri and Usipetes whom they were entertaining, had prepared for flight, left their country with all their belongings, and hidden themselves in the recesses of the forests.

Caesar remained a few days in their country, burned all their villages and homesteads, cut down their corn, and returned to the territory of the Ubii. Promising to help them in case they were molested by the Suevi, he ascertained from them that the latter, on learning from their scouts that the bridge was being made, had called a council according to their custom, and sent messengers in all directions, bidding the people to abandon the strongholds, convey their wives and children and all their belongings into the forests, and assemble— all of them who could bear arms—at a fixed place, nearly in the center of the region occupied by the Suevi; here they were awaiting the arrival of the Romans, and here they had determined to fight a decisive battle. Caesar had achieved every object for which he had determined to lead his army across,—overawed the Germans, punished the Sugambri, and relieved the Ubii from hostile pressure: he felt that honor was satisfied and that he had served every useful purpose. When, therefore, he heard the news about the Suevi, he returned to Gaul, having spent just eighteen days on the further side of the Rhine, and destroyed the bridge.

Only a small part of the summer remained, and in these parts, the whole of Gaul having a northerly trend, winter sets in early: nevertheless Caesar made active preparations for an expedition to Britain; for he knew that in almost all the operations in Gaul our enemies had been reinforced from that country. Besides, if there were not time for a campaign, he thought that it would be well worth his while merely to visit the island, see what the people were like, and make himself acquainted with the features of the country, the harbors, and the landing-places; for of all this the Gauls knew practically nothing. No one, indeed, readily undertakes the voyage to Britain except traders; and even they know nothing of it except the coast and the parts opposite the different regions of Gaul. Accordingly, though Caesar summoned traders from all parts to meet him, he could not ascertain the extent of the island, what tribes dwelt therein, their strength, their method of fighting, their manners and customs, or what harbors were capable of accommodating a large flotilla.

To procure information on these points before risking the attempt, he sent Gaius Volusenus, whom he considered perfectly competent, with a galley, instructing him to make a thorough reconnaissance and return as soon as possible. At the same time he marched with his whole force for the country of the Morini, as the shortest passage to Britain was from their coast, and ordered ships to assemble there from all the adjacent districts, as well as the fleet which he had built in the previous summer for the war with the Veneti. Meanwhile his envoys reported by traders to the Britons, whereupon envoys came to him from several tribes of the island, promising to give hostages and to submit to the authority of the Roman People. On hearing what they had to say, Caesar graciously reassured them, and sent them home, enjoining them to abide by their resolve. Along with them he sent Commius, whom, after the overthrow of the Atrebates, he had set up as king over that people,—a man of whose energy and judgement he had a high opinion, whom he believed to be loyal, and who was reputed to have great influence in the country. He instructed him to visit all the tribes he could, to urge them to trust to the good faith of the Roman People, and to announce that Caesar would soon arrive. Volusenus reconnoitered all the features of the coast, as far as he could get the chance, for he could not venture to disembark and trust himself to the natives, and in five days returned to Caesar and reported his observations.

While Caesar was waiting in these parts to get his ships ready for sea, envoys came from a large section of the Morini to apologize for their recent conduct in attacking the Roman People and promise obedience to his commands, pleading that they were uncivilized and knew nothing of our ways. Caesar regarded this as most opportune, for he had no wish to leave an enemy in his rear; owing to the time of year, he had no means of undertaking a campaign; and he did not think it wise to postpone his expedition to Britain for trivia. Accordingly he ordered the envoys to furnish a large number of hostages, and on their arrival admitted the Morini to terms. About eighty transports, which he considered sufficient to convey two legions, were collected and assembled; the galleys which he had besides he assigned to the quaestor, the generals, and the auxiliary officers. Besides these there were eighteen transports, eight miles off, which were prevented from making the same harbor by contrary winds: these he assigned to the cavalry. Placing the rest of the army under the command of two generals, Quintus Titurius Sabinus and Lucius Aurunculeius Cotta, with orders to march against the Menapii and those clans of the Morini from which no envoys had come, he directed another general, Publius Sulpicius Rufus, to hold the port with a force which he considered adequate.

The arrangements were now complete; and, taking advantage of favourable weather, he set sail about the third watch, directing the cavalry to march to the further harbor, embark there, and follow him. They were rather dilatory in getting through their work; but Caesar, with the leading ships, reached Britain about this fourth hour; and there, standing in full view on all the heights, he saw an armed force of the enemy. The formation of the ground was peculiar, the sea being so closely walled in by abrupt heights that it was possible to throw a missile from the ground above on to the shore. Caesar thought the place most unsuitable for landing, and accordingly remained till the ninth hour, waiting at anchor for the other ships to join him. Meanwhile he assembled the generals and tribunes, told them what he had learned from Volusenus, and explained his own plans, charging them to bear in mind the requirements of war and particularly of seamanship, involving as it did rapid and irregular movements, and to see that all orders were carried out smartly and at the right moment. The officers dispersed; and, getting wind and tide together in his favor, Caesar gave the signal, weighed anchor, and, sailing on about seven miles further, ran the ships aground on an open and shelving shore.

The natives knew what the Romans intended. Sending on ahead their cavalry and charioteers—a kind of warriors whom they habitually employ in action—they followed with the rest of their force and attempted to prevent our men from disembarking. It was very difficult to land, for these reasons. The size of the ships made it impossible for them to ground except in deep water; the soldiers did not know the ground, and with their hands loaded, and weighted by their heavy, cumbrous armor, they had to jump down from the ships, keep their foothold in the surf, and fight the enemy all at once; while the enemy had all their limbs free, they knew the ground perfectly, and standing on dry land or moving forward a little into the water, they threw their missiles boldly and drove their horses into the sea, which they were trained to enter. Our men were unnerved by the situation; and having no experience of this kind of warfare, they did not show the same dash and energy that they generally did in battles on land.

Caesar, noticing this, ordered the galleys, with the look of which the natives were not familiar, and which were easier to handle, to sheer off a little from the transports, row hard and range alongside of the enemy's flank, and slingers, archers, and artillery to shoot from their decks and drive the enemy out of the way. This maneuver was of great service to our men; for the natives, alarmed by the build of the ships, the motion of the oars, and the strangeness of the artillery, stood still, and then drew back a little. And now, as our soldiers were hesitating, chiefly because of the depth of the water, the standard-bearer of the 10th, praying that his attempt might redound to the success of the legion, cried, "Leap down, men, unless you want to abandon the eagle to the enemy: I, at all events, shall have done my duty to my country and my general." Uttering these words in a loud voice, he threw himself overboard, and advanced, bearing the eagle, against the enemy. Then, calling upon each other not to suffer such a disgrace, the men leaped all together from the ship. Seeing this, their comrades in the nearest ships followed them, and advanced close up to the enemy.

Both sides fought with spirit; but the Romans, being unable to keep their ranks unbroken or get firm foothold or follow their respective standards, and, as they came from this or that ship, joining any standard they met, became greatly confused; while the enemy knew all the shallows, and when from their standpoint on shore they saw a few men disembarking one by one, urged on their horses, and, surrounding the little group in numbers, attacked them before they were ready; others again got on the exposed flank of an entire company and plied them with missiles. Caesar, noticing this, ordered the men-of-war's boats and also the scouts to be manned, and, whenever he saw any of his men in difficulties, sent them to the rescue. Our men, as soon as they got upon dry land, followed by all their comrades, charged the enemy and put them to flight, but could not pursue them far because the cavalry had not been able to keep their course and make the island. This was the only drawback to Caesar's usual good fortune.

The beaten enemy at once sent envoys to Caesar to sue for peace, promising to give hostages and to obey his commands. The envoys were accompanied by the Atrebatian, Commius, who, as I have already related, had been sent on by Caesar to Britain in advance. He had just landed, and, in the character of an envoy, was conveying Caesar's mandates to the Britons, when they seized him and loaded him with chains; but now, after the battle, they sent him back, and, while suing for peace, laid the blame of the outrage upon the rabble, and begged that it might be overlooked in consideration of their ignorance. Caesar complained that, after the Britons had spontaneously sent envoys to the continent and asked him for peace, they had attacked him without provocation, but said that he would pardon their ignorance, and demanded hostages. Part of the required number they handed over at once, saying that they had to fetch the rest from long distances, and would deliver them in a few days. Meanwhile they ordered their followers to go back to their districts, while chiefs began to come in from all parts and place themselves and their tribes under Caesar's protection.

Peace had been thus established, when, dispersed by three days after the expedition reached Britain, the eighteen ships, mentioned above, which had taken the cavalry on board, sailed from the upper port with a light breeze. They were getting close to Britain and were seen from the camp, when such a violent storm suddenly arose that none of them could keep their course, but some were carried back to the point from which they had started, while the others were swept down in great peril to the lower and more westerly part of the island. They anchored notwithstanding, but as they were becoming waterlogged, were forced to stand out to sea in the face of night and make for the continent.

The same night it happened to be full moon, which generally causes very high tides in the Ocean, a fact of which our men were not aware. The result was that the galleys, in which Caesar had brought over troops, and which he had drawn up on dry land, were waterlogged, while the transports, which were at anchor, were damaged by the storm, and the men were unable to be of any service or go to their assistance. Several ships were wrecked; the rest were rendered useless by the loss of their rigging, anchors, and other fittings; and naturally the whole army was seized by panic. There were no other ships to take them back; everything required for repairing ships was lacking; and, as the troops all understood that they would have to winter in Gaul, no corn for the winter had been provided on the spot.

When this became known, the British chiefs who had waited on Caesar after the battle took counsel together. They knew that the Romans had neither cavalry nor ships nor grain; and they gathered that their troops were few from the smallness of the camp, which, as Caesar had taken over the legions without heavy baggage, was extraordinarily contracted. They therefore concluded that their best course would be to renew hostilities, cut off our men from corn and other supplies, and protract the campaign till winter, being confident that, if they overpowered them or prevented their return, no invader would ever again come over to Britain. Accordingly they renewed their oaths of mutual fidelity, and began to move away one by one from the camp and to fetch their tribesmen secretly from the districts.

Caesar was not yet aware of their plans; but from what had happened to his ships and from the fact that the chiefs had left off sending hostages, he guessed what was coming. Accordingly he prepared for all contingencies. He had corn brought in daily from the fields into camp; utilized the timber and bronze belonging to the ships that had been most severely damaged to repair the rest; and ordered everything required for the purpose to be brought over from the continent. The men worked with hearty goodwill; and, thus although twelve ships were lost, he managed to have the rest made tolerably seaworthy.

Meanwhile a legion, the 7th, was sent out in the ordinary course to fetch corn. So far no one had suspected that hostilities were brewing; for some of the natives still remained in the districts, while others were actually passing in and out of the camp; but the troops on guard in front of the gates of the camp reported to Caesar that an unusual amount of dust was to be seen in the direction in which the legion had gone. Suspecting (with good reason, as it happened) that the natives had hatched some scheme, Caesar ordered the cohorts on guard to accompany him in the direction indicated, two of the others to relieve them, and the rest to arm and follow him immediately. He had advanced some little distance from the camp when he observed that his troops were hard pressed by the enemy and could barely hold their own, the legion being huddled together and missiles hurled in from all sides. All the corn had been cut except in this one spot; and the enemy, anticipating that the Romans would come here, had lain in wait in the woods during the night; then, when the troops had laid aside their weapons and were dispersed and busy reaping, they had suddenly fallen upon them. A few were killed; the rest, whose ranks were not properly formed, were thrown into confusion; and the enemy's horse and war-chariots had at the same time encompassed them.

First of all the charioteers drive all over the field, the warriors hurling missiles; and generally they throw the enemy's ranks into confusion by the mere terror inspired by their horses and the clatter of the wheels. As soon as they have penetrated between the troops of cavalry, the warriors jump off the chariots and fight on foot. The drivers meanwhile gradually withdraw from the action, and range the cars in such a position that, if the warriors are hard pressed by the enemy's numbers, they may easily get back to them. Thus they exhibit in action the mobility of cavalry combined with the steadiness of infantry; and they become so efficient from constant practice and training that they will drive their horses at full gallop, keeping them well in hand, down a steep incline, check and turn them in an instant, run along the pole, stand on the yoke, and step backwards again to the cars with the greatest nimbleness.

Our men were unnerved by these movements, because the tactics were new to them; and Caesar came to their support in the nick of time. When he came up the enemy stood still, and our men recovered from their alarm. Thinking, however, that the moment was not favourable for challenging the enemy and forcing on a battle, he simply maintained his position, and after a short interval withdrew the legions into camp. During these operations our people were all busy, and the rest of the Britons, who were still in their districts, left them. Stormy weather followed for several days running, which kept the troops in camp and prevented the enemy from attacking. Meantime the natives sent messengers in all directions, telling their tribesmen that our troops were few, and pointing out that they had an excellent opportunity for plundering and establishing their independence for good by driving the Romans from their camp. By these representations they speedily got together a large body of horse and foot, and advanced against the camp.

Caesar foresaw that what had happened on previous days would happen again,—even if the enemy were beaten, their mobility would enable them to get off scot free; however, he luckily obtained about thirty horsemen, whom the Atrebatian, Commius, already mentioned, had taken over with him, and drew up the legions in front of the camp. A battle followed; and the enemy, unable to stand long against the onset of our troops, turned and fled. The troops pursued them as far as their speed and endurance would permit, and killed a good many of them; then, after burning all the buildings far and wide, they returned to camp.

On the same day the enemy sent envoys who came to Caesar to sue for peace. He ordered them to find twice as many hostages as before and take them across to the continent; for the equinox was near, and, as his ships were unsound, he did not think it wise to risk a stormy passage. Taking advantage of favourable weather, he set sail a little after midnight. All the ships reached the continent in safety; but two transports were unable to make the same harbors as the rest, and drifted a little further down.

About three hundred infantry had landed from these two vessels and were making the best of their way to camp, when the Morini, who had troops whom had been quite submissive when Caesar left them on attacked by hope of plunder, and told them, if they did not want to be killed, to lay down their arms. The Morini were not very numerous at first; but when the soldiers formed square and defended themselves, about six thousand, hearing the uproar, quickly assembled. On receiving the news, Caesar sent all his cavalry from camp to rescue his men. Meanwhile our soldiers sustained the enemy's onslaught and fought most gallantly for more than four hours; a few of them were wounded, but they killed many of their assailants. After our cavalry came in sight, the enemy threw away their arms and fled, and a large number of them were cut to pieces.

Next day Caesar sent Titus Labienus, in command of the legions which he had brought back from Britain, to punish the rebellious Morini. The marshes, which had served them as a refuge in the previous year, were dried up; and having no place to escape to, almost all of them fell into the hands of Labienus. Quintus Titurius and Lucius Cotta, the generals who had led the other legions into the country of the Menapii, finding that they had all taken refuge in the thickest parts of their forests, ravaged all their lands, cut their corn, burned their homesteads, and returned to Caesar, who quartered all the legions for the winter in the country of the Belgae. Thither no more sent hostages: the rest neglected to do so. In honor of these achievements, the Senate, on receiving Caesar's dispatches, appointed a thanksgiving service of twenty days.

BOOK V

Caesar's second invasion of Britain—The disaster at Aduatuca—
Quintus Cicero at bay—The doom of Indutiomarus

When Caesar, according to his yearly custom, was leaving his winter quarters for Italy, in the consulship of Lucius Domitius and Appius Britain, he ordered the generals whom he had placed in command of the legions to have as many ships as possible built during the winter and the old ones repaired. He explained the principle and indicated the lines on which they were to be built. To enable them to be loaded rapidly and hauled up on shore, he had them made a little shallower than those which are habitually used in the Mediterranean, (especially as he had found that, owing to the frequent ebb and flow of the tides, the waves there are comparatively small). On the other hand, to carry stores as well as the numerous horses, he built them a little wider than those which we use in other waters. All these vessels he ordered to be constructed both for rowing and sailing, which was greatly facilitated by their low freeboard, and the tackle required for fitting them out to be imported from Spain. After finishing the assizes in Cisalpine Gaul, he started for Illyricum, hearing that the Pirustae were making devastating raids upon the adjacent part of the province. On his arrival, he levied troops from the tribes and ordered them to concentrate at a prescribed place. The Pirustae, on hearing of this, sent envoys to tell him that the authorities were not responsible for anything that had occurred, and declared themselves ready to make full reparation. After listening to what the envoys had to say, Caesar ordered them to furnish hostages, who were to be brought to him by a fixed date, warning them that, in default of compliance, he would attack the tribe. The hostages were brought punctually, in obedience to his orders; and he appointed umpires to weigh the matters in dispute between the several tribes and settle the fines.

After disposing of these affairs and finishing the assizes, Caesar returned to Cisalpine Gaul, and thence started to join the army. On his arrival, he inspected all the camps, and found that, thanks to the extraordinary energy of the troops, and notwithstanding the extreme deficiency of resources, about six hundred ships of the class described above and twenty-eight galleys had been built, and would be ready for launching in a few days. Heartily commending the soldiers and the officers who had superintended the work, he gave the necessary instructions, and ordered all the ships to assemble at the harbor, from which he had ascertained that the passage to Britain was most convenient—the run from the continent being about thirty miles. Leaving an adequate number of troops to effect this movement, he started with four legions in light marching order and eight hundred horse for the country of the Treveri, as they would not attend his councils or submit to his authority, and were said to be making overtures to the Germans.

This tribe possesses by far the most power in the whole of Gaul, as well as numerous infantry; and, as we have remarked above, its territory reaches the Rhine. Two rivals, Indutiomarus and Cingetorix, were engaged in a struggle for supremacy. The latter, as soon as the approach of Caesar and his legions was known, presented himself before him, gave an assurance that he and all his followers would remain staunch and not break off their friendship with the Romans, and told him what was going on among the Treveri. Indutiomarus, on the other hand, proceeded to levy horse and foot and to make preparations for war, while he sent those who were not of an age to bear arms into the Ardennes, a forest of vast extent, which stretches from the Rhine through the heart of the Treveran territory to the frontier of the Remi. Some leading men, however, of the former tribe, influenced by friendship for Cingetorix and alarmed by the arrival of our army, came to Caesar and, feeling unable to do anything for their country, began to proffer petitions on their own behalf. Thereupon Indutiomarus, afraid of being left in the lurch, sent envoys to Caesar to say that he had only refrained from leaving his followers and presenting himself before him in order to keep the tribe loyal, lest, if all the men of rank left them, the masses, in their ignorance, might fall away. Accordingly the people were under his control, and, if Caesar would allow him, he would wait upon him in his camp and entrust his own interests and those of the community to his protection.

He spoke to him kindly and urged him to remain staunch. Nevertheless he summoned the leading men of the Treveri, and called upon them individually to support Cingetorix. He felt that Cingetorix deserved this service at his hands, and at the same time he thought it most important that a man of whose remarkable goodwill towards himself he had clear evidence should, as far as possible, command the respect of his own countrymen. Indutiomarus bitterly resented this action as diminishing his own credit; and, whereas he had already been ill-disposed towards us, this grievance kindled his indignation into a fiercer flame.

After settling these affairs, Caesar moved with the legions to the Italian harbor. There he learned that sixty ships, which had been built in the country of the Meldi, had been driven back by stress of weather, and, failing to keep their course, had returned to the point from which they had started: the rest he found completely fitted out and ready for sea. Some four thousand cavalry from the whole of Gaul and the leading men from all the tribes assembled at the same place. A few of them, of whose fidelity he was assured, he had determined to leave in Gaul, taking the rest with him as hostages, as he was afraid that, during his absence, there would be disturbances in the country.

Amongst the other hostages was Dumnorix, of whom we have already spoken. Caesar had determined to keep this man particularly under his eye, because he knew him to be an ardent revolutionary, fond of power, a man of masterful character, and possessing great influence with the Gauls. Moreover, Dumnorix had stated in the Aeduan council that Caesar was going to confer upon him the sovereignty over the tribe; and the Aedui were seriously offended at this remark, and yet did not venture to send envoys to Caesar to protest or to deprecate his intention. Caesar had learned this from natives who were his friends. Dumnorix at first earnestly prayed for leave to remain in Gaul; partly on the ground that he was not accustomed to being on board ship and dreaded the sea, partly, as he alleged, because he was debarred by religious obligations. Finding that his request was steadily refused and that there was no hope of getting Caesar's consent, he began to importune the Gallic magnates, taking them aside one by one and urging them to remain on the continent: he wrought upon their fears; he told them that there was some strong reason for robbing Gaul of all her men of rank; Caesar shrank from putting them to death under the eyes of their countrymen, but his purpose was to take them all over to Britain and there murder them. He made them promise to stay, and called upon them to swear that they would unite in carrying out the policy which they saw to be for the interest of Gaul. These intrigues were reported to Caesar by numerous informants. Having learned the facts, he determined, inasmuch as it was his policy to treat the Aedui with special distinction, that it was his duty to coerce and intimidate Dumnorix by every means in his power; and, as his frenzy was evidently passing all bounds, to see that he did no injury to himself personally or to the public interest.

For about twenty-five days he was kept waiting in the port, because the north-west wind, which commonly blows throughout a great part of the year on these coasts, made it impossible to sail. Accordingly he did his best to keep Dumnorix steady, but at the same time to acquaint himself with all his plans: at length, taking advantage of favourable weather, he ordered the infantry and cavalry to embark. While everybody's attention was distracted, Dumnorix, accompanied by the Aeduan cavalry, left the camp without Caesar's knowledge, and started for his own country. On receiving the news, Caesar broke off his departure, postponed all his arrangements, and sending a strong detachment of cavalry to pursue Dumnorix, ordered him to be brought back, and, in case he resisted and refused to submit, to be put to death; for he thought that a man who disregarded his authority when he was present would not behave rationally in his absence. When called upon to return he resisted, defended himself with vigor, and adjured his retainers to be true to him, crying loudly and repeatedly that he was a free man and belonged to a free people. The cavalry, in obedience to orders, surrounded the fellow and put him to death; the Aeduan cavalry all returned to Caesar.

Having disposed of this business, Caesar, leaving Labienus on the continent with three legions and two thousand cavalry to protect the ports, provide for a supply of corn, to ascertain what was passing in Gaul, and act as the circumstances of the moment might dictate, set sail towards sunset with five legions and the same number of cavalry as he had left behind. A light southwesterly breeze wafted him on his way: but about midnight the wind dropped; he failed to keep his course; and, drifting far away with the tide, he descried Britain at daybreak lying behind on the port quarter. Then, following the turn of the tide, he rowed hard to gain the part of the island where, as he had learned in the preceding summer, it was best to land. The energy shown by the soldiers on this occasion was most praiseworthy; rowing hard without a break they kept up in their heavily-laden transports with the ships of war. The ships all reached Britain about midday, but no enemy was visible: large numbers, as Caesar found out afterwards from prisoners, had assembled at the spot, but, alarmed by the great number of the ships, more than eight hundred of which, counting those of the preceding year and the private vessels which individuals had built for their own convenience, were visible at once, they had quitted the shore and withdrawn to the higher ground. Caesar disembarked the army and chose a suitable spot for a camp. Having ascertained from prisoners where the enemy's forces were posted, he left ten cohorts and three hundred cavalry near the sea to protect the ships, and marched against the enemy about the third watch. He felt little anxiety for the ships, as, he was leaving them at anchor on a nice open shore. The ships and the detachment which protected them were placed under the command of Quintus Atrius.

After a night march of about twelve miles Caesar descried the enemy's force. Advancing with their cavalry and chariots from higher ground towards a river, they attempted to check our men and force on an action. Beaten off by the cavalry, they fell back into the woods and occupied a well-fortified post of great natural strength, which they had apparently prepared for defense some time before with a view to intestine war, for all the entrances were blocked by felled trees laid close together. Fighting in scattered groups, they threw missiles from the woods, and tried to prevent our men from penetrating within the defenses; but the soldiers of the 7th legion, locking their shields over their heads, and piling up lumber against the defenses, captured the position and drove them out of the woods at the cost of a few wounded. Caesar, however, forbade them to pursue the fugitives far, partly because he had no knowledge of the ground, partly because much of the day was spent and he wished to leave time for entrenching his camp.

On the following morning he sent a light force of infantry and cavalry, in three columns, to pursue the fugitives. They had advanced a considerable distance, the rearguard being just in sight, when some troopers from Quintus Atrius came to Caesar with the news that there had been a great storm on the preceding night, and that almost all the ships had been damaged and gone ashore, as the anchors and cables did not hold, and the seamen and their captains could not cope with the force of the storm. The collisions between different vessels had therefore caused heavy loss. On receiving this information, Caesar recalled the legions and cavalry, ordering them to damage, defend themselves as they marched, and went back himself to the ships. He saw with his own eyes much the same as he had learned from the messengers and the dispatch which they brought: about forty ships were lost, but it seemed possible to repair the rest, though at the cost of considerable trouble. Accordingly he selected skilled workmen from the legions and ordered others to be sent for from the continent, at the same time writing to tell Labienus to build as many ships as possible with the legions under his command. Although it involved great trouble and labour, he decided that the best plan would be to have all the ships hauled up and connected with the camp by one entrenchment. About ten days were spent in these operations, the troops not suspending work even in the night. As soon as the ships were hauled up and the camp strongly fortified, Caesar left the same force as before to protect them, and advanced to the point from which he had returned. By the time that he had arrived reinforcements of Britons had assembled on the spot from all sides. The chief command and the general direction of the campaign had been entrusted by common consent to Cassivellaunus, whose territories are separated from those of the maritime tribes by a river called the Thames, under about eighty miles from the sea. He had before been incessantly at war with the other tribes; but in their alarm at our arrival the Britons had made him commander-in-chief.

The island is triangular in shape, one side being opposite Gaul. One corner of this side, by Kent—the landing-place for almost all ships from Gaul—has an easterly, and the lower one a southerly aspect. The extent of this side is about five hundred miles. The second trends westward towards Spain: off the coast here is Ireland, which is considered only half as large as Britain, though the passage is equal in length to that between Britain and Gaul. Half-way across is an island called Man; and several smaller islands also are believed to be situated opposite this coast, in which, according to some writers, there is continuous night, about the winter solstice, for thirty days. Our inquiries could elicit no information on the subject, but by accurate measurements with a water-clock we could see that the nights were shorter than on the continent. The length of this side, according to the estimate of the natives, is seven hundred miles. The third side has a northerly aspect, and no land lies opposite it; its corner, however, looks, if anything, in the direction of Germany. The length of this side is estimated at eight hundred miles. Thus the whole island is two thousand miles in circumference.

By far the most civilized of all the natives are the inhabitants of Kent—a purely maritime district—whose culture does not differ much from that of the Gauls. The people of the interior do not, for the most part, cultivate grain, but live on milk and flesh-meat and clothe themselves with skins. All the Britons, without exception, stain themselves with *woad*, which produces a blueish tint; and this gives them a wild look in battle. They wear their hair long, and shave the whole of their body except the head and the upper lip. Groups of ten or twelve men have wives in common, brothers generally sharing with each other and fathers with their sons; the offspring of these unions are counted as the children of the man to whose home the mother, as a virgin, was originally taken.

The enemy's horsemen and charioteers kept up a fierce running fight with our cavalry, the latter, however, getting the best of it at all points, and driving the enemy into the woods and on to the hills: they killed a good many, but, pursuing too eagerly, lost some of their own number. After a time, while our men were off their guard and occupied in entrenching their camp, the enemy suddenly dashed out of the woods, swooped down upon the outpost in front of the camp, and engaged in a hot combat; and when Caesar sent two cohorts—the first of their respective legions—to the rescue, which were separated from each other by a very small interval, our men were unnerved by tactics which were new to them, and they boldly charged between the two and got back unhurt. Quintus Laberius Durus, a military tribune, was killed that day. After additional cohorts had been sent up, the enemy were beaten off.

Throughout this peculiar combat, which was fought in full view of every one and actually in front of the camp, it was clear that the infantry, owing to the weight of their armor, were ill fitted to engage an enemy of this kind; for they could not pursue him when he retreated, and they dared not abandon their regular formation: also that the cavalry fought at great risk, because the enemy generally fell back on purpose, and, after drawing our men a little distance away from the legions, leaped down from their chariots and fought on foot with the odds in their favor. On the other hand, the mode in which their cavalry fought exposed the Romans, alike in retreat and in pursuit, an exactly similar danger. Besides, the Britons never fought in masses, but in groups separated by wide intervals; they posted reserves and relieved each other in succession, fresh vigorous men taking the places of those who were tired.

Next day the enemy occupied a position on the heights at a distance from the camp, and began to show themselves in scattered groups and harass our cavalry, but with less vigor than the day before. At midday, however, Caesar having sent three legions and all his cavalry on a foraging expedition under one of his generals, Gains Trebonius, they suddenly swooped down from all points on the foragers, not hesitating to attack the ordered ranks of the legions. The men charged them vigorously, beat them off, and continued to pursue them until the cavalry, relying upon the support of the legions, which they saw behind them, drove them headlong: they killed a great many of them and never allowed them to rally or make a stand or get down from their chariots. After this rout the reinforcements, which had assembled from all sides, immediately dispersed; and from that time the enemy never encountered us in a general action.

Having ascertained the enemy's plans, Caesar led his army to the Thames, into the territories of Cassivellaunus. The river can only be forded at one spot, and there with difficulty. On the passage reaching this place, he observed that the enemy were drawn up in great force near the opposite bank of the river. The bank was fenced by sharp stakes planted along its edge; and similar stakes were fixed under water and concealed by the river. Having learned these facts from prisoners and deserters, Caesar sent his cavalry on in front, and ordered the legions to follow them speedily; but the men advanced with such swiftness and dash, though they only had their heads above water, that the enemy, unable to withstand the combined onset of infantry and cavalry, quitted the bank and fled.

Cassivellaunus, abandoning, as we have remarked above, all thoughts of regular combat, disbanded the greater part of his force, retaining only about four thousand charioteers; watched our line of march; and, moving a little away from the track, concealed himself in impenetrable wooded spots, and removed the cattle and inhabitants from the open country into the woods in those districts through which he had learned that we intended to march. Whenever our cavalry made a bold dash into the country to plunder and devastate, he sent his charioteers out of the woods (for he was familiar with every track and path), engaged the cavalry to their great peril, and by the fear which he thus inspired prevented them from moving far afield. Caesar had now no choice but to forbid them to move out of touch with the column of infantry, and, by ravaging the country and burning villages, to injure the enemy as far as the legionaries' powers of endurance would allow.

Meanwhile the Trinovantes — about the strongest tribe in that part of the country—sent envoys to Caesar, promising to surrender and obey his commands. Mandubracius, a young chief of this tribe, whose father had been their king and had been put to death by Cassivellaunus, but who had saved his own life by flight, had gone to the continent to join Caesar, and thrown himself upon his protection. The Trinovantes begged Caesar to protect Mandubracius from harm at the hands of Cassivellaunus, and to send him to rule over his own people with full powers. Caesar sent Mandubracius, but ordered them to furnish forty hostages and grain for his army. They promptly obeyed his commands, sending hostages to the number required and also the grain.

As the Trinovantes had been granted protection and immunity from all injury on the part of the soldiers, the Cenimagni, Segontiaci, Ancalites, Japtire of Bibroci, and Cassi sent embassies to Caesar and surrendered. He learned from the envoys that the stronghold of Cassivellaunus, which was protected by woods and marshes, was not far off, and that a considerable number of men and of cattle had assembled in it. The Britons apply the name of stronghold to any woodland spot, difficult of access and fortified with a rampart and trench, to which they are in the habit of resorting in order to escape a hostile raid. Caesar marched to the spot indicated with his legions, and found that the place was of great natural strength and well-fortified; nevertheless he proceeded to assault it on two sides. The enemy stood their ground a short time, but could not sustain the onset of our infantry, and fled precipitately from another part of the stronghold. A great quantity of cattle was found in the place, and many of the garrison were captured as they were trying to escape, and killed.

While the operations above mentioned were going on in this district, Cassivellaunus sent envoys to Kent, which, as we have remarked above, is close to the sea, ordering Cingetonix, Carvilius, Taximagulus, and Segovax, the four kings who ruled over the country, to collect all their forces, make a sudden descent upon the naval camp, and attack it. When they reached the camp, the officers made a sortie, killed many of them, captured their leader Lugotorix, a man of rank, and withdrew their men without loss. On receiving news of the action, Cassivellaunus, who was greatly alarmed by the defection of the tribes, following the numerous disasters which he had sustained and the ravaging of his country, availed himself of the mediation of the Atrebatian, Commius, and sent envoys to Caesar to propose surrender. Caesar had resolved to winter on the continent, because disturbances were likely to break out suddenly in Gaul: not much of the summer remained, and the enemy, as, he knew, could easily spin out the time. Accordingly he ordered hostages to be given, and fixed the tribute which Britain was to pay annually to the Roman People, at the same time strictly forbidding Cassivellaunus to molest Mandubracius or the Trinovantes.

On receiving the hostages, he led back the army to the sea, where he found the ships repaired. When they were launched, he arranged to take the army back in two trips, as he had a large number of prisoners and some ships had been destroyed by the storm. It so happened that of all this numerous fleet, after so many voyages, not a single vessel conveying troops was lost either in this or in the preceding year; while of the ships that were empty, comprising those which had landed troops after the first trip and were sent back to Caesar from the continent, and sixty others which Labienus had constructed after the wreck, only a very few reached their destination, nearly all the rest being driven back. Caesar waited for them a considerable time in vain; and then, for fear the lateness of the season (just before the equinox) should prevent his sailing, he was obliged to pack the troops rather closely. A dead calm followed, and unmooring at the beginning of the second watch, he reached land at dawn and brought all the ships safe ashore.

The harvest that year in Gaul had been scanty on account of drought; and accordingly, after beaching the ships and holding a council of quarters over the Gallic deputies at Samarobriva, Caesar was compelled to quarter the army for the winter on a different principle from that which he had followed in former years, distributing the legions among several tribes. He assigned one of them to Gaius Fabius, one of his generals, another to Quintus Cicero, and a third to Lucius Roscius, with orders to march them into the countries of the Morini, the Nervii, and the Esuvii respectively; quartered the fourth under Titus Labienus in the country of the Remi, just on the frontier of the Treveri; and stationed three in Belgium under the command of the quaestor, Marcus Crassus, and two generals, Lucius Munatiis Plancus and Gaius Trebonius. A single legion, which he had recently raised north of the Po, was sent, along with five cohorts, into the country of the Eburones, a people ruled by Ambiorix and Catuvolcus, the greater part of whose territory is between the Meuse and the Rhine. Quintus Titurius Sabinus and Aurunculeius Cotta were ordered to take command of these troops. This method of distributing the legions Caesar regarded as the easiest way of remedying the scarcity of corn. And in fact the quarters of all the legions, except the one which he had sent under Lucius Roscius into a perfectly tranquil and undisturbed district, were enclosed within an area whose extreme points were only one hundred miles apart. Caesar determined to remain himself in Gaul until he ascertained that the legions were in their several positions and their camps entrenched.

Among the Carnutes was a man of noble birth, named Tasgetius, whose ancestors had held sovereignty in their own country, and to whom Caesar, in recognition of his energy and devotion (for in all his campaigns he had found his services exceptionally valuable), had restored their position. He was now in the third year of his reign when his enemies, with the avowed sanction of many of the citizens, assassinated him. The crime was reported to Caesar. Fearing that, as many were implicated, the tribe might be impelled by them to revolt, he ordered Lucius Plancus to march rapidly with his legion from Belgium into the country of the Carnutes, winter there, and arrest the individuals whom he found responsible for Tasgetius's death. Meanwhile he was informed by all the officers under whose command he had placed the legions, that they had reached their respective quarters and that the positions were entrenched.

About fifteen days after the positions had been taken up a sudden and alarming revolt was voiced, started by Ambiorix and Catuvolcus. They had waited upon Sabinus and Cotta at the frontier of their kingdom and conveyed the corn to the camp when, egged on by emissaries from the Sabinus, roused their tribesmen, suddenly overpowered a party who were cutting wood, and came with a large force to attack the camp. Our men speedily armed and mounted the rampart; some Spanish horse were sent out from one side and came off victorious in a cavalry combat; and the enemy, seeing the futility of their attempt, called off their troops. Then, after the manner of their nation, they shouted for someone on our side to go out and parley with them, declaring that they had something to say, affecting both sides, which, they hoped, might settle disputes.

Gaius Arpineius, a Roman knight, who was intimate with Quintus Titunus, was sent to confer with them, accompanied by one Quintus Ambiorix Junius, a Spaniard, who had been in the habit of visiting as Caesar's representative, troops to Ambiorix addressed them in the following terms. He would admit that he was deeply indebted to Caesar for various acts of kindness, having by his good offices been relieved of tribute which he had regularly paid to his neighbors, the Aduatuci, while his own son and his brother's, who had been sent to them as hostages and by them enslaved and imprisoned, had been sent back by Caesar; moreover, in attacking the camp, he had not acted spontaneously or on his own judgement, but under the compulsion of the tribe, his sovereignty being so far limited that the multitude had no less power over him than he over them. Furthermore, the tribe had only taken up arms because it was unable to resist a sudden conspiracy on the part of the Gauls. This he could easily prove from his own insignificance; for he was not so ignorant of affairs as to imagine that his troops could get the better of the Roman People. Gaul, however, was unanimous:

that very day had been fixed for a general attack on Caesar's camps, to prevent any one legion from assisting another. It was not easy for Gauls to refuse help to their countrymen, especially as the object of the movement was, of course, to recover national liberty. However, having done his duty to them on the score of patriotism, he now thought of what he owed to Caesar for his favors; he therefore urged, nay, implored, Titurius, as a friend whose salt he had eaten, to consider his own and his soldiers' safety. A large force of German mercenaries had crossed the Rhine, and would be at hand in a couple of days. It was for the Roman generals to decide whether they would withdraw their troops from camp before the neighboring tribes could find out, and transfer them either to Cicero or to Labienus, the former of whom was about fifty miles off, the latter rather more. He would solemnly promise on oath to grant them a safe-conduct through his territory. In so doing he was acting in the interests of his tribe, which would be relieved from the burden of the camp, and showing his gratitude for Caesar's services. After this speech Ambiorix withdrew.

Arpineius and Junius reported to the generals what they had heard. The suddenness of the news made them anxious; and although it came from an enemy, they did not think it wise to disregard it. What most alarmed them was that it seemed hardly credible that an obscure and insignificant tribe like the Eburones would have ventured to make war upon the Roman People on their own account. Accordingly they referred the question to a council of war, and a violent dispute arose between them. Lucius Aurunculeius and many of the tribunes and chief centurions held that it would not be right to take any step without due consideration or to leave the camp without authority from Caesar. They pointed out that, as the camp was fortified, it was possible to hold out against any force, even of Germans. Experience proved this; for they had resolutely sustained the enemy's first onslaught and inflicted heavy loss upon him into the bargain; they were not pressed for supplies; and reinforcements would arrive in time from the nearest camp and from Caesar himself: finally, what could be more puerile or more unsoldierlike than to make a momentous decision on the advice of an enemy.

In opposition to these arguments, Titurius loudly insisted that it would be too late to act when the enemy's reinforcements had arrived with their German allies, or the nearest camp had suffered a disaster. The time for deliberation was short. Caesar, so he believed, had started for Italy; otherwise the Carnutes would not have dreamed of putting Tasgetius to death; nor, if Caesar had been at hand, would the Eburones have held our men so cheap as to attack the camp. It was not to the enemy that he looked for guidance, but to facts. The Rhine was close by. The Germans were embittered by the death of Ariovistus and our earlier victories; Gaul was ablaze with indignation at all the indignities she had suffered, at her subjection to the dominion of the Roman People, and at the eclipse of her former military renown. Finally, who could persuade himself that Ambiorix had ventured upon an enterprise like this without solid support? His advice was safe either way: if nothing untoward happened, they would get to the nearest legion without any danger; if the whole of Gaul were in league with the Germans, their only safety was in prompt action. As to Cotta and those who took the opposite view, what would be the result of following their counsel? It involved, if not immediate danger, at all events the prospect of a long blockade accompanied by famine.

Such were the arguments on both sides; and, as Cotta and the chief centurions continued to oppose him vehemently, Sabinus, raising his voice, so that a large number of the soldiers might hear, cried, "Have your own way, if you like. Death has no more terrors for me than for you. The men will judge; and if any disaster happens, they'll call you to account for it; whereas if you, Cotta, would consent, on the day after tomorrow they would join their comrades in the nearest camp and share the fortune of war with them, instead of perishing by the sword or by famine, like outcasts far removed from their fellows."

The assembled officers stood up. Sabinus took the two generals by the hand and implored them not to precipitate a disaster by quarrelling and obstinacy; go or stay, everything could be managed if only they were all unanimous; but no good, that they could see, would come from quarrelling. The dispute dragged on till midnight. At length Cotta, overborne by superior authority, gave way: Sabinus's view prevailed. An order was issued that the troops were to march at daybreak. The men stayed up for the rest of the night, every one looking about to see what he could take with him, what part of his winter's kit he would be forced to leave behind. Men thought of every argument to persuade themselves that they could not remain without danger, and that the danger would be increased by protracted watches and consequent exhaustion. At dawn they marched out of camp.

The enemy, perceiving from the hum of Ambiorix's voices in the night and the Romans remaining the column, stationed themselves in ambush in two divisions in the woods, in a convenient position, screened from observation, about two miles off, to await their arrival; and when the bulk of the column had moved down into a large defile, they suddenly showed themselves on either side of it, hustled forward the rearguard, checked the ascent of the van, and forced on a combat on a spot most unfavorable for our men.

And now Titurius, having exercised no forethought, lost all nerve, ran from place to place, and tried to get the cohorts into formation; but he did this nervously and in such a way that one could see he was at his wits' end, as indeed generally happens to men who are forced to decide on the spur of the moment. Cotta, on the other hand, who had foreseen, that these things might happen on the march, and for that reason had declined to sanction the movement, was fully equal to the occasion : he performed a general's part in calling upon the men and encouraging them, and in action he did the work of a private soldier. Owing to the length of the column, it was not easy for the generals to look to everything themselves and make the necessary arrangements for every part of the field; they therefore ordered the word to be given to abandon the baggage and form in a square. Although, in the circumstances, the plan cannot be condemned, its effect was nevertheless disastrous; for, as it would evidently not have been resorted to but for extreme anxiety and despair, it made our soldiers despondent and stimulated the enemy's ardor for battle. Moreover, as was inevitable, soldiers were everywhere abandoning their companies, every one hurrying to the baggage-train to look for his most cherished possessions and carry them off; while the whole field was a scene of weeping and uproar.

The natives, on their part, showed no lack of resource. Their leaders ordered the word to be passed along the line that no man was to stir from his post: the booty was their prize, and whatever the Romans left was to be kept for them. They were to remember, then, that everything depended upon victory. Our men were as brave as they and not overmatched in point of numbers: forsaken by their leader and by fortune, they trusted for safety to courage alone; and as often as a cohort charged, there many of the enemy fell. Observing this, Ambiorix ordered the word to be given for the tribesmen to throw their missiles from a distance and not go too close; wherever the Romans charged, they were to fall back: being lightly armed and in constant training, they could not suffer; when the Romans attempted to rejoin their companies, they were to pursue.

The order was carefully obeyed. Whenever a cohort left the square and charged, the enemy ran swiftly away. Meanwhile the cohort was necessarily exposed, and missiles fell on its unshielded flank. When the men began to return to the position they had left, they were surrounded by the enemy who stood near them as well as by those who had fallen back: if, on the other hand, they chose to hold their ground, there was no room for courage; and, being crowded together, they could not avoid the missiles hurled by that huge host. Yet, harassed by all these disadvantages and in spite of heavy loss, they held out; and throughout a combat which lasted the greater part of the day, from dawn till the eighth hour, they did nothing unworthy of themselves. At this moment Titus Balventius, who, in the previous year, had been chief centurion of his legion—a brave and highly-respected man— had both his thighs pierced by a javelin; Quintus Lucanius, an officer of the same rank, while trying to save his son, who had been surrounded, was killed, fighting most gallantly; and Lucius Cotta, while cheering on all the cohorts and centuries, was struck full in the face by a stone from a sling.

Quintus Titurius was greatly agitated at the aspect of affairs; and descrying Ambiorix some way off haranguing his men, he sent his interpreter, Gnaeus Pompeius, to ask for quarter for himself and the troops. In reply to this appeal, Ambiorix said that Titurius might speak to him if he liked; he hoped that the host might be induced to consent as far as the safety of the troops was concerned: Titurius, at all events, should come to no harm, and for that he would pledge his word. Sabinus consulted the wounded Cotta, proposing that, if he approved, they should withdraw from the action and together confer with Ambiorix, who might, he hoped, be induced to spare both them and the troops. Cotta replied that he would not meet an armed enemy; and to this resolve he adhered.

Sabinus ordered the tribunes and centurions whom he had round him at the moment to follow him. On approaching Ambiorix, he was ordered to lay down his arms, and obeyed, telling his officers to do the same. The principals were discussing about terms, and Ambiorix was purposely making a long speech, when Sabinus was gradually surrounded and slain. Then, in the native fashion, they shouted "Victory," and with a loud yell dashed into our ranks and broke them. Lucius Cotta fell fighting where he stood, and the bulk of the men with him. The rest retreated to the camp, whence they had come. Lucius Petrosidius, the standard-bearer, finding himself beset by a multitude of enemies, threw his eagle inside the rampart, and, fighting most gallantly in front of the camp, was slain. His comrades with difficulty sustained the onslaught till night: then, seeing that hope was gone, they all slew each other to the last man. A few, who had slipped away from the battle, made their way by the woodland tracks to the quarters of Titus Labienus and told him what had occurred.

Ambiorix was in high glee at his victory. Bidding his infantry follow him, he started at once with his cavalry for the country of the Aduatuci, who were conterminous with his kingdom, and pushed on throughout the night and the next day. Having related what had happened and roused the Aduatuci, he reached the country of the Nervii next day, and urged them not to lose the chance of establishing their independence for good and taking vengeance upon the Romans for the wrongs which they had suffered. Two generals, he told them, were killed, and a great part of the army had perished: there would be no difficulty in surprising the legion that was wintering under Cicero and destroying it. He promised to help in the attack, and the Nervii were readily persuaded by his words.

Accordingly they at once sent off messengers to the Ceutrones, Grudii, Levaci, Pleumoxii, and Geidumni, all of whom are under their sway, raised as large a force as they could, and swooped down unexpectedly upon Cicero's camp before the news of Titunus's death reached him. In his case too the inevitable result was that some soldiers who had gone off into the forests to fetch wood for fortification were cut off by the sudden arrival of the cavalry and surrounded; and the Eburones, Nervii, and Aduatuci, accompanied by all their allies and dependents, attacked the legion in great force. Our men flew to arms and mounted the rampart. They could barely hold out that day, for the enemy staked all their hopes upon swift action; and they were confident that if they were victorious on this occasion, their victory would be lasting.

Cicero instantly sent dispatches to Caesar, offering large rewards to the messengers if they succeeded in delivering them; but all the roads were blocked, and the messengers were intercepted. In the night as many as one hundred and twenty towers were run up with incredible speed out of the timber which the men had collected for fortification; and the defects in the works were made good. Next day the enemy, who had been largely reinforced, renewed their attack on the camp, and filled up the trench. Our men resisted in the same way as the day before; and day after day the course of events was the same. Work went on without a break throughout the night: neither the sick nor the wounded could get a chance of rest. Everything necessary for repelling the next day's attack was got ready in the night: numerous stakes, burnt and hardened at the ends, and a large number of heavy pikes were prepared; the towers were furnished with platforms, and embattled breastworks of wattle-work were fastened to them. Cicero himself, though he was in very poor health, would not allow himself to rest even in the nighttime; so that the soldiers actually thronged round him and by their remonstrances constrained him to spare himself.

And now the commanders and chieftains of the Nervii, who had some claim to address Cicero and were on friendly terms with him, expressed the wish to have an interview. Their request being granted, they repeated the same tale that Ambiorix had told in dealing with Titurius: the whole of Gaul was in arms; the Germans had crossed the Rhine; Caesar's camp and the camps of the other officers were beleaguered. They also mentioned the death of Sabinus, and pointed to Ambiorix to gain credit for their story. The Romans, they said, were mistaken if they expected any help from men who were themselves desperate. However, they had no quarrel with Cicero and the Roman People, except that they objected to winter camps and did not want the custom to become established: they might leave their camp in safety, as far as they were concerned, and go wherever they liked, without fear.

To these arguments Cicero simply replied that it was not the habit of the Roman People to accept terms from an armed enemy: if the Gauls would lay down their arms, they could send envoys to Caesar and avail themselves of his intercession; Caesar was just, and he hoped that they would obtain what they asked.

After this rebuff the Nervii invested the Roman siege camp with a rampart ten feet high and a trench fifteen feet wide. They had learned the secret from observing our methods in former years; and they also got hints from prisoners whom they had taken, belonging to our army: but, as they had no supply of iron tools suitable for the purpose, they were obliged to cut the sods with their swords, and take up the earth with their hands and in their cloaks. From this one could form an estimate of their vast numbers; for in less than three hours they completed a contravallation three miles in extent; and during the next few days they proceeded, after due preparation, to construct towers proportioned to the height of the Roman rampart, grappling-hooks, and sappers' huts, which the prisoners had also taught them how to make.

On the seventh day of the siege a great a desperate gale sprang up; and the besiegers began to sling resolutely red-hot bullets made of plastic clay and to throw burning darts at the huts, which, in the Gallic fashion, were thatched. The huts quickly took fire, and, owing to the force of the wind, the flames spread all over the camp. The enemy cheered loudly, as if victory were already certain, and began to move forward their towers and huts and to escalade the rampart. But so great was the courage of the legionaries, and such was their presence of mind, that, although they were everywhere scorched by the flames and harassed by a hail of missiles, and knew that all their baggage and everything that belonged to them was on fire, not only did none of them abandon his post on the rampart, but hardly a man even looked round; and in that hour all fought with the utmost dash and resolution. This was far the most trying day for our men; but nevertheless the result was that a very large number of the enemy were killed or wounded, for they had crowded right under the rampart, and the rear ranks would not allow those in front to fall back. The fire abating a little, a tower was pushed up at one point and brought into contact with the rampart, when the centurions of the 3rd cohort stepped back from the spot where they were standing, withdrew all their men, and began to challenge the enemy, by voice and gesture, to come on if they liked; but not one of them dared to advance. Then they were sent flying by showers of stones from every side; and the tower was set on fire.

In this legion there were two centurions, Pullo and Vorenus, who, by dint of extraordinary courage, were getting close to the first grade. They were forever disputing as to which was the better man; and every year they contended for promotion with the greatest acrimony. When the fighting at the entrenchment was at its hottest, "Vorenus," cried Pullo, "why hesitate? What better chance can you want of proving your courage? This day shall settle our disputes." With these words he walked outside the entrenchment, and where the enemy's ranks were thickest dashed in. Vorenus of course did not keep inside the rampart: afraid of what every one would think, he followed his rival. At a moderate distance, Pullo threw his javelin at the enemy and struck one of them as he was charging out of the throng: he fainted from the blow, and the enemy protected him with their shields, and all together hurled their missiles at his assailant and cut off his retreat. Pullo's shield was transfixed, and the dart stuck in his sword-belt. The blow knocked his scabbard round, so that his hand was hampered as he tried to draw his sword; and in his helpless state the enemy thronged round him. His rival, Vorenus, ran to his rescue, and helped him in his stress. In a moment the whole multitude left Pullo, believing that the dart had killed him, and turned upon Vorenus. Sword in hand, Vorenus fought at bay, killed one of his assailants, and forced the rest a little way back; but pressing on too eagerly, he ran headlong down a slope and fell. He was in his turn surrounded, but Pullo succoured him, and the two men slew several of the enemy and got back, safe and sound and covered with glory, into the entrenchment. Thus Fortune made them her puppets in rivalry and combat, rival helping rival and each saving the other, so that it was impossible to decide which was to be deemed the braver man.

Day by day the perils and the hardships of the siege increased, for this reason above all, a dispatch to that, many of the soldiers being enfeebled by wounds, few were now available for defense; and day by day messengers were sent off with dispatches to Caesar in more and more rapid succession. Some of them were caught and tortured to death in sight of our soldiers. There was a solitary Nervian in the camp, named Vertico, a man of good birth, who at the beginning of the siege had taken refuge with Cicero, and had done him loyal service. This man induced his slave, by the hope of freedom and by large rewards, to take a dispatch to Caesar. The slave carried the dispatch tied to a javelin, and, being a Gaul himself, went among the Gauls without exciting any suspicion, and made his way to Caesar, who learned from him the perils that encompassed Cicero and the legion.

Caesar received the dispatch about the eleventh hour. He at once sent a messenger the rescue, to Marcus Crassus, the quaestor, whose camp was twenty-five miles off, ordering his legion to march at midnight and join him speedily. Crassus left on receiving the message. Caesar sent another messenger to Gaius Fabius, bidding him march his legion into the country of the

Atrebates, through which he knew that he would himself have to go, and wrote to Labienus, directing him, if he could do so consistently with the public interest, to move with his legion to the country of the Nervii. As the rest of the army was rather too far off, he did not think it wise to wait for it; but he got together about four hundred horsemen from the nearest camps.

About the third hour he learned from the scouting parties of Crassus's advanced guard that he was coming, and on the same day marched twenty miles. He left Crassus in command at Samarobriva, and assigned him a legion, as he was leaving behind the heavy baggage of the army, the hostages of the various tribes, the state papers, and the whole of the grain which he had brought there to last the winter. Fabius obeyed orders, and, without any serious delay, joined Caesar on the march with his legion. Labienus was aware of the fate of Sabinus and the massacre of his cohorts; the whole host of the Treveri was upon him; and he was afraid that, if he quitted his camp like a runaway, he would not be able to sustain the enemy's attack, especially as he knew that they were elated by their recent success; accordingly he sent a dispatch to Caesar, telling him that it would be very dangerous for him to withdraw his legion from its quarters, describing what had happened in the country of the Eburones, and explaining that the whole host of the Treveri, horse and foot, had taken up a position three miles from his camp.

Caesar approved his decision; and although he had only two legions instead of the three which he had expected, he saw that success was just possible with speed. By forced marches he advanced into the Nervian territory, where, learning from prisoners what was going on at Cicero's camp, and realizing the extreme peril of his position, he induced one of his Gallic horsemen to carry a letter to him. He wrote it in Greek characters, for fear it might be intercepted and his plans become known to the enemy, and advised the man, if he could not get into the camp, to tie the letter to the thong of a javelin and throw it inside the entrenchment. He said that he had started with his legions and would soon arrive, and exhorted Cicero to be true to himself. The Gaul, dreading the risk of detection, threw his javelin, as he had been directed. It chanced to lodge in a tower and was not noticed by our men for two days; but on the third day a soldier observed it, took it down, and brought it to Cicero. After perusing the letter, he paraded the troops and read it aloud, to their intense delight. And now the smoke of distant fires was seen; and all doubt about the coming of the legions was dispelled.

The Gauls, on hearing the news from their patrols, raised the siege, and marched to the valley.

Cavalry skirmishes took place that day by the water-side, but the two armies maintained their respective positions, the Gauls waiting for reinforcements, which had not yet come up, while Caesar hoped that he might perhaps succeed, by feigning fear, in enticing the enemy over to his position, and thus be able to fight on the near side of the valley, in front of his camp; or, failing that, might reconnoiter the roads and so cross valley and rivulet with less risk. At daybreak the enemy's horse came close up to the camp and engaged ours. Caesar deliberately ordered his cavalry to give way and fall back into the camp, at the same time directing the troops to increase the height of the rampart on all sides and block up the gateways, and in doing so to move about as hurriedly as possible and do their work with a pretense of fear.

Lured on by all these devices, the enemy crossed over and formed up on unfavorable ground; and as our men were actually withdrawn from the rampart, they ventured nearer, and threw missiles from all sides into the entrenchment, sending round criers with orders to announce that if any one, Gaul or Roman, cared to come over and join them before the third hour, he might safely do so, but that after that time the permission would be withdrawn. The gates were blocked, but merely for show, with a single row of sods; and, fancying that they could not break through that way, some of them, in their contempt for our men, began to demolish the rampart with their bare hands, and others to fill up the ditches. Then, while the infantry rushed out from all the gates, Caesar let loose the cavalry and quickly sent the enemy flying, not a man standing to strike one blow. Many were slain, and all had to drop their arms.

Caesar was afraid to continue the pursuit, because there were woods and marshes in the way, and he could see no chance of inflicting the smallest loss upon the fugitives; but he reached Cicero on the same day without the loss of a man. He surveyed with admiration the towers which the enemy had erected, their sappers' huts, and earthworks: when the legion was paraded, he found that not one man in ten had got off unwounded; and from all these things he appreciated the danger and the resolution with which the defense had been conducted. Warmly commending Cicero for his services, and also the legion, he addressed individually the centurions and tribunes, who, as he learned from Cicero's report, had shown distinguished gallantry. Having obtained correct information from prisoners about the fate of Sabinus and Cotta, he paraded the legion next day, described what had happened, and cheered and reassured the men:—the culpable rashness of a general officer had entailed a disaster; but they must take it calmly, for the blessing of the immortal gods and their own valour had repaired the loss; and the enemy had as little cause for lasting exultation as they for inordinate grief.

Meanwhile the news of Caesar's victory was brought to Labienus with incredible rapidity: he was sixty miles from Cicero's camp, and it was past the ninth hour when Caesar arrived there; yet before midnight a shout arose at the gates of his camp, announcing a victory and conveying the congratulations of the Remi. When the news reached the Treveri, Indutiomarus, who had determined to attack Labienus's camp on the following day, made off in the night and withdrew his whole force into their country. Caesar sent back Fabius and his legion to camp, intending to winter himself with three legions in three separate camps near Samarobriva; and, as such serious disturbances had broken out in Gaul, he determined to remain with the army the whole winter. When the news of Sabinus's calamitous death spread abroad, almost all the tribes of Gaul began to form warlike projects, sending messages and embassies in all directions, trying to ascertain each other's plans and see who would take the initiative, and holding meetings by night in lonely places. Caesar indeed had hardly any respite all through the winter from the harassing expectation of hearing news about schemes and outbreaks on the part of the Gauls. Among the reports which reached him was one from Lucius Roscius, whom he had placed in command of the 13th legion, announcing that large numbers of Gauls had assembled from the Armorican tribes, as they are called, to attack him, and had been within eight miles of his camp, but that, on receiving the announcement of Caesar's victory, they had made off like runaways.

Caesar summoned the leading men of each tribe to his presence; frightened some by letting them know that he was aware of what was going on; encouraged others; and thus managed to keep a large part of Gaul obedient. The government of the Senones, however, an extremely powerful tribe, who have great influence among the Gauls, attempted to put to death Cavarinus, whom Caesar had set over them as king, and whose brother, Moritasgus, had held sovereignty when Caesar came to Gaul, and his ancestors before him. Cavarinus, anticipating their design, had fled. They pursued him as far as the frontier, dethroned and banished him, and then sent envoys to Caesar to explain. He ordered the whole council to appear before him; but they refused to obey. The mere fact that leaders had been found to strike the first blow had so much weight with the ignorant natives, and wrought such a complete change in the temper of all, that, except the Aedui and the Remi, whom Caesar always treated with special distinction— the former in consideration of their long-standing and steady loyalty to the Roman People, the latter for their recent services in the war—there was hardly a single tribe that we did not suspect. And indeed I am inclined to think that their conduct was quite natural, for this reason among many others:—the Gauls were once the most warlike of all people; and it was most bitterly mortifying to them to have so completely lost that reputation as to be forced to submit to the domination of the Roman People through the winter, without intermission. The Treveri and Indutiomarus continued sending envoys across the Rhine, making overtures to tribes, promising them money, and assuring them that the greater part of our army had been destroyed and that the existent was insignificant. Not a single German tribe, however, could be induced to cross the Rhine: they said that they had tried twice—in the war with Ariovistus and the migration of the Tencteri— and would not tempt fortune any more. Not-withstanding this disappointment, Indutiomarus proceeded to raise forces and drill them, to procure horses from the neighboring peoples, and by large rewards to induce exiles and condemned criminals from the whole of Gaul to join him. Indeed, he had now acquired such prestige in the country by these measures that embassies poured in from all quarters, soliciting his countenance and alliance both privately and with the authority of their respective governments.

Finding that advances were being spontaneously made to him, that on one side there were the Senones and Carnutes, stimulated by consciousness of guilt, on the other the Nervii and Aduatuci, preparing to attack the Romans, and that once he made a forward movement outside his frontier, he would have no lack of volunteers, he gave notice of a muster in arms. This, by Gallic usage is tantamount to a declaration of war. By intertribal law all adult males are obliged to attend the muster under arms; and the last comer is tortured to death in sight of the host. At this gathering Indutiomarus passed judgement upon Cingetorix, the leader of the rival party, his own son-in-law (who, as we have already observed, had thrown in his lot with Caesar and had not failed him), declaring him a public enemy, and confiscated his property. After this step, he announced before the assembled host that he had been invited by the Senones, the Carnutes, and several other tribes to join them, and intended to march through the territory of the Remi, ravaging their lands, but first of all to attack the camp of Labienus. He then gave the necessary orders. Labienus, who was ensconced in a strongly fortified camp of great natural strength, felt no anxiety for himself or his legion: his only care was not to lose any chance of striking a decisive blow. Accordingly, having ascertained from Cingetorix and his relations the drift of Indutiomarus's speech at the gathering, he sent messengers to the neighboring tribes and summoned cavalry from all sides, naming a date for their arrival. Meanwhile Indutiomarus rode up and down almost every day close under the rampart of the camp, sometimes to examine the position, sometimes to converse with or intimidate the soldiers; while all his troopers generally threw missiles inside the rampart. Labienus steadily kept his men within the entrenchment, and did everything in his power to foster the belief that he was cowed.

Day after day Indutiomarus moved up to the camp with growing contempt. Labienus made the cavalry, which he had summoned from all the neighboring tribes, enter the entrenchment in a single night, and was so careful to keep all his troops inside under guard that it was quite impossible for their arrival to be made public or reach the knowledge of the Treveri. Meanwhile Indutiomarus, according to his daily custom, came up to the camp and spent a great part of the day there, his troopers throwing missiles and challenging our men in the most insulting terms to fight. The men made no reply; and towards evening, thinking it time to be off, they broke up and dispersed. Suddenly Labienus sent out orders that when the enemy were panic-stricken and routed, as he rightly foresaw would happen, all ranks were to look out for Indutiomarus, and not a man strike a blow till he saw Indutiomarus killed; for he resolved that he should not gain time to escape by delay with the rest. He set a heavy price upon his head, and sent a number of cohorts to support the cavalry. Fortune justified the general's plans. With every man on his track, Indutiomarus was caught and killed in the act of fording a river, and his head brought back to camp. The cavalry on their way back pursued and killed all they could. On learning what had happened, the forces of the Eburones and Nervii which had assembled all went off; and thenceforward Caesar found Gaul somewhat more peaceable.

BOOK VI

Continued disturbances in north-eastern Gaul – Caesar's second passage of the Rhine – Manners and customs, religions and institutions of the Gauls and Germans – Ill-omened Aduatuca – Extermination of the Eburones

Anticipating, for many reasons, increased disturbances in Gaul, Caesar determined to employ his lieutenants, Marcus Silanus, Gaius Antistius Reginus, and Titus Sextius, in raising troops. At the same time he requested Gnaeus Pompeius, then proconsul, who, though vested with the command of an army, remained, on public grounds, in the neighborhood of the capital, to order the recruits from Cisalpine Gaul whom he had sworn in, when consul, to join their standards and repair to his quarters; for, looking to the future as well as the present, he thought it essential, with a view to impressing public opinion in Gaul, that the resources of Italy should appear sufficient not only to repair speedily any disaster in the field, but actually to increase the original army. Pompeius acceded to this request from motives of patriotism as well as of friendship: the levy was speedily completed by Caesar's officers; and thus before the close of winter three legions were organized and mobilized, making double the number of the cohorts lost under Quintus Titurius. By this swift display of armed force he showed what could be affected by the organization and resources of the Roman People.

After the death of Indutiomarus, already described, his command was transferred to his relations, who tried persistently to gain the support of the neighboring German rebellious peoples by promises of money. Failing to obtain the Nervii, a favourable answer from their neighbors, they made overtures to the more distant tribes, and found some compliant. The parties mutually confirmed the alliance by oath, and hostages were given as security for the money; at the same time the Treveri made a formal alliance with Ambiorix. On learning this, Caesar felt it necessary to take the field at once, for he saw that warlike preparations were afoot on all sides. The Nervii, the Aduatuci, and the Menapii, combined with all the local Germans, were in arms; the Senones refused to attend at his bidding, and were in communication with the Carnutes and the neighboring peoples; while the Treveri were sending embassies in rapid succession to solicit the aid of the Germans.

Accordingly, before the winter was over, Caesar assembled the four nearest legions, made an unexpected raid into the country of the Nervii, and, before they could either concentrate or flee, captured a large number of cattle and also of men, handed over this booty to the troops, ravaged the country, and compelled the Nervii to surrender and give hostages. This affair rapidly disposed of, he withdrew the legions once more into winter quarters. In the early spring he convened a Gallic council, as usual. All the delegates, except the Senones, Carnutes, and Treveri, attended; and, regarding their absence as the first step in rebellion, he determined to mark his sense of its paramount importance, and accordingly transferred the council to Lutetia, a town belonging to the Parisii. The Parisii were conterminous with the Senones, and the two had, within recent times, formed one state; but on this occasion were believed to have dissociated themselves from the Senones. After announcing the adjournment from the front of the tribunal in his camp, Caesar started on the same day with his legions for the country of the Senones, and made his way thither by forced marches. The ringleader of the conspiracy, on learning his approach, directed the populace to assemble in the forts. They endeavored to obey; but before they could do so the arrival of the Romans was announced. Compelled to abandon their intention, they sent envoys to entreat Caesar's forbearance, who were introduced by the Aedui, under whose protection their tribe had been from time immemorial. At the request of the Aedui, Caesar readily pardoned them and accepted their excuses, feeling that the summer-time should be devoted to the impending war, not to investigation. He ordered them, however, to find a hundred hostages, whom he handed over to the custody of the Aedui. The Carnutes likewise sent envoys and hostages to Caesar's quarters, availing themselves of the intercession of the Remi, whose dependents they were, and received the same answer. Caesar then finished the business of the council, and directed the tribes to furnish cavalry.

Having tranquillized this part of Gaul, he devoted himself, heart and soul, to the campaign against the Treveri and Ambiorix. He directed Cavarinus to take the cavalry of the Senones and accompany him, for fear any disturbance should arise among the tribe from his resentment or from the odium which he had brought upon himself. After making these arrangements, he endeavored to fathom Ambiorix's intentions, for he regarded it as certain that he did not intend to fight. Close to the country of the Eburones, and protected by continuous marshes and forests, were the Menapii, the only people in Gaul who had never sent envoys to Caesar to sue for peace. He knew that they were on friendly terms with Ambiorix; and he had ascertained that they had also, through the medium of the Treveri, come to an understanding with the Germans. His idea was to deprive Ambiorix of the support of these tribes before attacking him, lest, in despair, he should take refuge in the country of the Menapii, or be driven to join the peoples beyond the Rhine. Having decided upon this plan, he sent the heavy baggage of the whole army into the country of the Treveri, to Labienus, and ordered two legions to join him; while he started in person with five legions in light marching order for the country of the Menapii. They had not assembled any force, but, relying upon the strength of their country, took refuge in the forests and marshes and transferred their belongings thither.

Caesar placed Gaius Fabius and the quaestor, Marcus Crassus, in command of divisions, and, rapidly constructing causeways, advanced with the three columns, burned homesteads and hamlets, and captured a large number of cattle and also of men. Yielding to this pressure, the Menapii sent envoys to him to sue for peace. He took hostages, from them, and warned them that he would treat them as enemies if they admitted either Ambiorix or his agents within their territories. After settling these affairs, he left the Atrebatian, Commius, with a body of cavalry as a warden among the Menapii, and marched in person for the country of the Treveri.

While Caesar was engaged in these operations, the Treveri, who had assembled a large force of infantry and cavalry, were preparing to attack Labienus and the single legion which was wintering in their country. They were within two days' march of his position when they learned that the two legions dispatched by Caesar had arrived. Encamping fifteen miles off, they determined to wait for reinforcements from the Germans. Labienus ascertained their intention, and, hoping that their rashness would give him an opportunity for bringing them to action, left five cohorts to guard his baggage, marched against the enemy with twenty-five cohorts and a large body of cavalry, and encamped within a mile of them. Between him and the enemy there was a river with steep banks, which was difficult to cross. He had no intention of crossing it himself, and did not think it likely that the enemy would do so. Their prospects of obtaining reinforcements were daily improving. Labienus remarked openly in a council of war that, as the Germans were said to be approaching, he would not risk his own reputation and the safety of his army, but would strike his camp next morning at dawn. His words rapidly reached the enemy; for out of a large body of Gallic cavalry it was naturally inevitable that some should sympathize with the Gallic cause. In the night Labienus called together the tribunes and chief centurions, explained his plans, and, with the view of making the enemy believe that he was afraid of them, ordered the camp to be struck with more noise and bustle than is customary with Romans. By this means he contrived that his departure should resemble a flight. This also was reported to the enemy by their patrols before daybreak; for the two camps were very close together.

The rearguard had barely got outside the entrenchment when the Gauls told each other not to let the hoped-for prize slip from their grasp: it would be waste of time to wait for German aid when the Romans were panic-stricken; and it was humiliating, with their huge host, to shrink from attacking a handful of men, especially as they were running away and hampered by their baggage. With this encouragement, they did not hesitate to cross the river and force on an action on unfavorable ground. Labienus had divined that this would happen, and hoping to lure them all across the stream, he kept quietly moving on, feigning, as before, that he was marching away. Then, sending on the baggage a little way and parking it on a knoll, "Soldiers," he said, "you have got your chance. You have the enemy in your grasp: he is in a bad position, where he is not free to act. Show the same courage under my command that you have shown many a time under the chief: imagine that he is here, watching what is going on." With these words he ordered the column to wheel into line of battle and advance, and, sending a few troops of horse to protect the baggage, posted the rest on the flanks. The men raised a cheer and swiftly launched their javelins against the enemy. Seeing the runaways unexpectedly advancing to attack them, they could not even sustain their charge, but the moment they closed, fled precipitately to the nearest woods. Labienus hunted them down with his cavalry, killed a large number, took numerous prisoners, and a few days afterwards received the submission of the tribe; for the Germans, who were on their way to reinforce the Treveri, hearing of their rout, went back home. The relations of Indutiomarus, who had started the revolt, followed in their train and fled the country. The chief authority was transferred to Cingetorix, who, as we have explained, had from the outset remained steadily loyal.

After his march from the country of the Menapii to that of the Treveri, Caesar determined to cross the Rhine, for two reasons:—first, because Caesar again had sent the Treveri reinforcements; and secondly, to prevent allies of Ambiorix from finding an asylum in their country. Accordingly he proceeded to construct a bridge a little above the spot where he had crossed before. The principle of construction was perfectly familiar; and by great energy on the part of the men, the work was completed in a few days. Leaving a strong guard by the bridge in the country of the Treveri, to prevent any sudden outbreak on their part, he transported the remaining forces, including the cavalry, across the river. The Ubii, who had previously given hostages and submitted, wishing to clear themselves, sent envoys to him to explain that no reinforcements had been sent from their country into that of the Treveri, and that they had not been guilty of disaffection: they earnestly begged him to spare them, and not to make the innocent suffer for the guilty through indiscriminate animosity against the Germans, promising to give more hostages, if he required them. On making inquiry he found that the reinforcements had been sent by the Suevi; accordingly he accepted the explanations of the Ubii and asked for particulars about the routes leading into the country of the Suevi.

A few days later he was informed by the Ubii that the Suevi were all concentrating their forces and warning the tribes under their sway to send their contingents of horse and foot. On receiving this information he arranged for a supply of grain and selected a suitable spot for a camp.

At the same time he directed the Ubii to withdraw their flocks and herds and transfer all their belongings from the open country into their strongholds, hoping that the ignorant barbarians might be tempted by want of food to fight a battle in unfavorable conditions; and he instructed them to send numerous scouts into the country of the Suevi and to ascertain what they were about. The Ubii fulfilled their instructions, and, after the lapse of a few days, reported that all the Suevi, on the arrival of messengers with trustworthy information about the Roman army, had retreated with all their forces and those which they had raised from their allies to the furthest extremity of their country, where there was an immense forest called Bacenis, stretching far into the heart of the continent, and, like a natural wall, protecting the Cherusci from the raids of the Suevi, and the Suevi from those of the Cherusci. On the outskirts of this forest the Suevi had determined to await the arrival of the Romans.

At the stage which this narrative has reached, it will not, I think, be irrelevant to describe the manners and customs of the Gauls and the Germans, and the points wherein the two peoples differ one from the other. Factions exist in Gaul, not only among all the tribes and in all the smaller communities and subdivisions, but, one may almost say, in separate households: the leaders of the rival factions are those who are popularly regarded as possessing the greatest influence; and accordingly to their judgement belongs the final decision on all questions and political schemes. This custom seems to have been established at a remote period in order that none of the common people might lack protection against the strong; for the rival leaders will not suffer their followers to be oppressed or overreached; otherwise they do not command their respect. The same principle holds good in Gaul regarded in its entirety, the tribes as a whole being divided into two groups.

When Caesar arrived in Gaul, one faction was headed by the Aedui, the other by the Sequani. The latter, being in themselves the weaker (for the supremacy had from time immemorial been vested in the Aedui, who possessed extensive dependencies), had secured the alliance of the Germans under Ariovistus, gaining their adhesion by lavish expenditure and promises. As a result of several victories, in which all the Aedui men of rank were killed, they had far outstripped their rivals in power, annexing a large proportion of their dependencies, taking the sons of their leading men as hostages, making the authorities swear to form no designs hostile to the Sequani, seizing and occupying a part of their territory near the common frontier, and establishing supremacy over the whole of Gaul. Yielding to the inevitable, Diviciacus had undertaken a journey to Rome, to solicit aid from the Senate, but had returned unsuccessful. On the arrival of Caesar, the situation was completely changed; the Aedui recovered their hostages, regained power supremacy; over their former dependents, and gained new ones through the influence of Caesar,—for the tribes who had allied themselves to them found that they were better off and more equitably treated than before,—while in other respects their influence and prestige were increased. The Sequaui, on the other hand, had lost their supremacy. Their place was taken by the Remi; and, as it was known that they stood as high in Caesar's favor as the Aedui, the tribes who could not be induced, on account of old feuds, to join the latter ranged themselves among the dependents of the Remi. The Remi took care to protect them, and thus secured the new authority which they had suddenly acquired. The situation at that time was this: the Aedui ranked far the highest in general estimation, while the Remi stood next to them in importance.

Everywhere in Gaul two classes only alone possess or enjoy any distinction; the masses are regarded almost as slaves, never venture to act on their own initiative, and are not admitted to any council. Generally, when masses, crushed by debt or heavy taxation or ill-treated by powerful individuals, they bind themselves to serve men of rank, who exercise over them all the rights that masters have over their slaves. One of the two classes consists of the Druids, the other of the Knights.

The former officiate at the worship of the gods, regulate sacrifices, private as well as public, and expound questions power of religion. Young men resort to them in large numbers for study, and the people hold them in great respect. They are judges in nearly all disputes, whether between tribes or individuals; and when a crime is committed, when a murder takes place, when a dispute arises about inherited property or boundaries, they settle the matter and fix the awards and fines. If any litigant, whether an individual or a tribe, does not abide by their decision, they excommunicate the offender, — the heaviest punishment which they can inflict. Persons who are under such a sentence are looked upon as impious monsters: everybody avoids them, everybody shuns their approach and conversation, for fear of incurring pollution; if they appear as plaintiffs, they are denied justice; nor have they any share in the offices of state. The Druids are all under one head, who commands the highest respect among the order. On his death, if any of the rest is of higher standing than his fellows, he takes the vacant place: if there are several on an equality, the question of supremacy is decided by the votes of the Druids, and sometimes actually by force of arms. The Druids hold an annual session on a settled date at a hallowed spot in the country of the Carnutes,—the reputed center of Gaul. All litigants assemble here from all parts and abide by their decisions and awards.

The Druids, as a rule, take no part in war, and do not pay taxes conjointly with other people: they enjoy exemption from military service and immunity from all burdens. Attracted by these great privileges, many persons voluntarily come to learn from them, while many are sent by their parents and relatives. During their novitiate it is said that they learn by heart a great number of verses; and accordingly some remain twenty years in a state of pupilage. It is against the principles of the Druids to commit their doctrines to writing, though, for most other purposes, such as public and private documents, they use Greek characters. Their motive, I take it, is twofold: they are unwilling to allow their doctrine to become common property, or their disciples to trust to documents and neglect to cultivate their memories; for most people find that, if they rely upon documents, they become less diligent in study and their memory is weakened. The doctrine which they are most earnest in inculcating is that the soul does not perish, but that after death it passes from one body to another: this belief they regard as a powerful incentive to valour, as it inspires a contempt for death. They also hold long discussions about the heavenly bodies and their motions, the size of the universe and of the earth, the origin of all things, the power of the gods and the limits of their dominion, and instruct their young scholars accordingly.

The second of the two classes consists of the Knights. On occasion, when war breaks out, as happened almost every year before Caesar's arrival, the Knights either attacking or repelling attack, they all take the field, and surround themselves with as many armed servants and retainers as their birth and resources permit. This is the only mark of influence and power which they recognize.

The Gallic people, in general, are remarkably addicted to religious observances; and for human sacrifices. For this reason persons suffering from serious maladies and those whose lives are danger offer or vow to offer human sacrifices, and employ Druids to perform the sacrificial rites; for they believe that unless the life of man be duly offered, the divine spirit cannot be propitiated. They also hold regular state sacrifices of the same kind. They have, besides, colossal images, the limbs of which, made of wicker-work, they fill with living men and set on fire; and the victims perish, encompassed by the flames.

They regard it as more acceptable to the gods to punish those who are caught in the commission of theft, robbery, or any other crime; but, in default of criminals, they actually resort to the sacrifice of the innocent.

The god whom they most reverence is Mercury, whose images abound. He is regarded as the inventor of all arts and the pioneer and guide of travelers; and he is believed to be all-powerful in promoting commerce and the acquisition of wealth. Next to him they reverence Apollo, Mars, Jupiter, and Minerva. Their notions about these deities are much the same as those of other peoples: Apollo they regard as the dispeller of disease, Minerva as the originator of industries and handicrafts, Jupiter as the suzerain of the celestials, and Mars as the lord of war. To Mars, when they have resolved upon battle, they commonly dedicate the spoils: after victory they sacrifice the captured cattle, and collect the rest of the booty in one spot. In the territories of many tribes are to be seen heaps of such spoils reared on consecrated ground; and it has rarely happened that any one dared, despite religion, either to conceal what he had captured or to remove what had been consecrated. For such an offence the law prescribes the heaviest punishment with torture.

The Gauls universally describe themselves as descendants of Dis Pater, affirming that this is the Druidical tradition. For this reason they measure all periods of time not by days but by nights, and reckon birthdays, the first of the month, and the first of the year on the principle that day comes after night. As regards the other customs of daily life, about the only point a peculiar in which they differ from the rest of mankind is this,—they do not allow their children to come near them openly until they are old enough for military service; and they regard it as unbecoming for a son, while he is still a boy, to appear in public where his father can see him.

It is the custom for married men to take dowries from their own property an amount equivalent, according to valuation, to the sum which they have received from their wives as dowry, and lump the two together. The whole property is jointly administered and the interest saved; and the joint shares of husband and wife, with the interest of past years, go to the survivor. Husbands have power of life and death over status of their wives as well as their children: on the death of the head of a family of high birth, his relations assemble, and, if his death gives rise to suspicion, examine his wives under torture, like slaves, and, if their guilt is proved, burn them to death with all kinds of tortures. Funerals, considering the Gallic standard of living, are splendid and costly: everything, even including animals, which the departed are supposed to have cared for when they were alive, is consigned to the flames; and shortly before our time slaves and retainers who were known to have been beloved by their masters were burned along with them after the conclusion of the regular obsequies.

The tribes which are regarded as comparatively well-governed have a legal enactment to the effect that if any one hears any political rumor or intelligence from the neighboring peoples, he is to inform the magistrate and not communicate it to anyone else, as experience has proved that headstrong persons, who know nothing of affairs, are often alarmed by false reports and impelled to commit crimes and embark on momentous enterprises. The magistrates suppress what appears to demand secrecy, and publish what they deem it expedient for the people to know. The discussion of politics, except in a formal assembly, is forbidden.

The manners and customs of the Germans differ widely from those just described. They have no Druids to preside over public worship. The Germans care nothing for sacrifices. The only deities whom they recognize are those whom they can see, and from whose power they derive manifest benefit, namely, Sun, Moon, and Fire: the rest they have not even heard of. Their lives are passed entirely in hunting and warlike pursuits; and from infancy they are inured to toil and hardship. Those who preserve their virginity longest are most respected by their fellows, for it is considered that by such continence stature and strength are developed and nerve invigorated: indeed, to have connection with a woman before her twentieth year is thought most disgraceful. Concealment is impossible, as they bathe promiscuously in rivers and only wear hides or small cloaks of reindeer skin, leaving a large part of the body bare.

The Germans are not an agricultural people, and live principally upon milk, cheese and meat. Nobody possesses any landed estate and have no or private demesne: the authorities and chieftains annually assign to the several clans and groups of kinsmen assembled at the time as much land as they think proper, in whatever quarter they please, and in the following year compel them to remove to another place. Many reasons are assigned for this custom:—that men may not become slaves of habit, lose their zest for war, and take to agriculture instead; that the strong may not aim at the acquisition of large estates and dispossess those of low degree; that they may not build with elaboration, to avoid cold and heat; to prevent the growth of avarice, which gives birth to party-spirit and dissension; and to keep the masses contented and therefore quiet by letting everyone see that he is as well off as the most powerful.

The greatest distinction which a tribe can have is to be surrounded by as wide a belt as possible of waste and desert land. They regard it as a tribute to their valour that the neighboring peoples should be dispossessed and retreat, and that no one should venture to settle in their vicinity; at the same time they count on gaining additional security by being relieved from the fear of sudden raids. When a tribe has to repel or to make an attack, officers are chosen to conduct the campaign and invested with powers of life and death. In time of peace there is no central magistracy: the chiefs of the various districts and hundreds administer justice and settle disputes among their own people. No discredit attaches to predatory expeditions outside the tribal boundary; and the people tell you that they are undertaken in order to keep the young men in training and to prevent laziness. Whenever any of the chiefs announces his intention in the assembly of leading an expedition, and calls for volunteers, those who approve the enterprise and the leader stand up and promise to help, and the whole gathering applaud them: those who do not follow their leader are counted as deserters and traitors, and thenceforth they are no longer trusted. To ill-treat a guest is regarded as a crime: those who visit them, from whatever motive, they shield from injury and regard their persons as sacred; every man's house is open to them, and they are welcomed at meals.

Once there was a time when Gauls were more warlike than Germans, actually invading their country and, on account of their dense population and insufficient territory, sending colonies across the Rhine. Thus they occupied the most fertile districts of Germany round the mans: their present Hercynian forest (which, I find, was known by degeneracy, name to Eratosthenes and other Greeks, who called it Orcynia), and there settled. To this day the people in question, who enjoy the highest reputation for fair dealing and warlike prowess, continue to occupy this territory. The Germans still live the same life of poverty, privation, and patient endurance as before, and their food and physical training are the same; while the Gauls, from the proximity of the provinces and familiarity with sea-borne products, are abundantly supplied with luxuries and articles of daily consumption. Habituated, little by little, to defeat, and beaten in numerous combats, they do not even pretend themselves to be as brave as their neighbors.

The Hercynian forest, above mentioned, extends over an area which a man travelling without encumbrance requires nine days to traverse. There is no other way of defining its extent, and the natives have no standards of measurement. Starting from the frontiers of the Helvetii, Nemetes, and Rauraci, it extends right along the line of the Danube to the frontiers of the Dacians and Anartes; then, bending to the left and passing through a country remote from the river, it borders (so vast is its extent) upon the territories of many peoples; and no one in Western Germany can say that he has got to the end of the forest, even after travelling right on for sixty days, or has heard whereabouts it begins. It is known to produce many kinds of wild animals which have never been seen elsewhere. The following, on account of their strongly marked characteristics, seem worthy of mention.

There is a species of ox, shaped like a stag, with a single horn standing out between its ears from the middle of its forehead, higher and straighter than horns as we know them spread out wide from the top, like hands and branches. The characteristics of the male and the female are identical, and so are the shape and size of their horns.

Again, there are elks, so-called, which resemble goats in shape and in having piebald coats, but are rather larger. They have blunt horns, and their legs have no knots or joints. They do not lie down to sleep; and if by any chance they are knocked down, they cannot stand up again, or even raise themselves. Their resting-places are trees, against which they lean, and thus rest in a partially recumbent position. Hunters mark their usual lair from their tracks, and uproot or cut deep into all the trees in the neighborhood, so that they just look as if they were standing. The animals lean against them as usual, upset the weakened trunks by their mere weight, and fall down along with them.

There is a third species, called aurochs, a little smaller than elephants, having the appearance, color, and shape of bulls. They are very strong and swift, and attack every man and beast they catch sight of. The natives sedulously trap them in pits and kill them. Young men engage in the sport, hardening their muscles by the exercise; and those who kill the largest head of game exhibit the horns as a trophy, and thereby earn high honor. These animals, even when caught young, cannot be domesticated and tamed. Their horns, in size, shape, and appearance, differ widely from those of our oxen. The natives, who are fond of collecting them, mount them round the rim with silver and use them as drinking-cups at grand banquets.

After ascertaining from the Ubian scouts that the Suevi had retreated into their forests, Caesar determined to advance no further. Germans, as we have explained above, pay very little attention to agriculture, and he was therefore afraid of running short of corn. Still, to avoid releasing the natives altogether from the fear of his return, and to delay their reinforcements, after withdrawing the army he broke down the end of the bridge, for the length of two hundred feet, which touched the Ubian bank, erected a tower with four stories on its extremity, and posted a detachment of twelve cohorts to protect the bridge, fortifying the position with strong works. A young officer, Gaius Volcacius Tullus, was placed in command, and charged with the defense of the position. Now that the crops were beginning to ripen, Caesar started in person to conduct the campaign against Ambiorix, taking the route through the Ardennes, the largest forest in the whole of Gaul, which extends from the banks of the Rhine — the Treveran frontier—to the country of the Nervii

—a distance of more than five hundred miles. He sent on ahead Lucius Minucius Basilus with all the cavalry, in the hope that by marching rapidly and so arriving in good time he might be able to strike an effective blow; enjoined him not to allow fires to be lighted in his camp, that there might be no distant sign of his approach; and promised to follow him immediately.

Basilus carried out his instructions. Making a rapid march, which upset all calculations, he surprised and seized a large number of men in the open country, and, following their directions, hastened to a place where Ambiorix himself with a few horsemen was said to be staying. Fortune is a great power in war, as in all other affairs. By a rare chance Basilus came upon Ambiorix himself when he was still off his guard and unprepared, and they all saw him coming before his approach was rumored or announced; and by great good luck, although all the equipment which he had with him was looted and his carriages and horses seized, Ambiorix himself escaped death. His escape, however, was partly due to the fact that his house, like the dwellings of the Gauls in general, was surrounded by a wood (for, in order to escape the heat, they generally look for sites near woods and rivers); and accordingly his retainers and friends resisted for a time, in this confined space, the onslaught of our horsemen. While they were fighting, one of his followers mounted him on horseback; and the woods covered his flight. Thus Fortune had much to do both with his peril and with his escape.

Whether Ambiorix deliberately stopped from collecting his forces in the belief that it would be unwise to fight, or whether his inaction was due to want of time and the sudden arrival of the cavalry, which made him believe that the rest of the army was following; is doubtful. At all events he sent out messengers over the countryside, bidding every man shift for himself. Some fled into the Ardennes, others to unbroken stretches of morass; those who lived nearest the Ocean hid themselves in districts periodically insulated by the tides. Many quitted their own country and trusted their lives and all that they possessed to utter strangers. Catuvolcus, who joined in the enterprise of Ambiorix, and was now a worn-out old man, unable to stand the hardships of campaigning or of flight, heartily cursed Ambiorix for having planned the enterprise, and poisoned himself with yew, a tree which grows abundantly in Gaul and Germany. The Segni and Condrusi, who are Germans by race and are reckoned among that people, and in charge of who dwell between the Eburones and the Treveri, sent envoys to Caesar, begging him not to count them as enemies or assume that all the Germans were associated, and assuring him that they had never dreamed of war, and had sent no reinforcements to Ambiorix. Caesar, after testing their statements by examining prisoners, ordered them to hand over to him any Eburonian fugitives who joined them, and promised not to molest their country if they obeyed. He then broke up his forces into three divisions, and transferred the heavy baggage of all the legions to Aduatuca (the name denotes a fort), in which Titurius and Aurunculeius had established themselves for the winter, and which is nearly in the center of the territory of the Eburones. Amongst other reasons, Caesar had selected the position in order to spare the soldiers fatigue, as the fortifications made in the preceding year were still standing. Leaving the 14th legion, one of the three which he had brought from Italy, where they had recently been raised, to protect the baggage, he entrusted Quintus Tullius Cicero with the command of it and the defense

After dividing the army, he ordered Titus and Labienus to move towards the Ocean with three legions into the districts bordering upon the country of the Menapii, and sent Gaius Trebonius with the same number, to devastate the region adjacent to the country of the Aduatuci; while he determined to march himself with the remaining three towards the river Scheldt, which flows into the Meuse, and the most distant parts of the Ardennes, whither he heard that Ambiorix had gone with a few horsemen. On his departure, he announced his intention of returning at the end of a week, when, as he was aware, the rations of the legions left on guard would be due. He enjoined Labienus and Trebonius to return by that day, if they could do so consistently with the public interest, so that, after comparing notes anew and ascertaining the enemy's methods, they might be able to form a fresh plan of campaign.

As we have remarked above, there was no organized body, no stronghold, and no force capable of armed resistance: the population was dispersed in all directions. Everyone had taken up his abode in any remote glen or wooded spot or impenetrable morass that offered him a chance of defending himself or of saving his life. The people near these places knew the ground; and great care was required, not indeed in protecting the army as a whole, for while the troops were massed no danger could befall them from a panic-stricken and scattered enemy, but to secure the safety of individual soldiers; and yet this in some measure concerned the safety of the whole army.

Lust for plunder led many far afield; and the woods with their ill-defined and dusky paths defied compact bodies to enter them. If Caesar meant to finish his task outright and slaughter the whole brood of scoundrels, he must send out numerous parties and break up the troops into detachments; if he chose to keep his companies in formation, according to the established and familiar system of the Roman army, the natives were protected by the nature of the country, and individuals among them had courage enough to lie in ambush and cut off scattered parties. In these difficult circumstances all possible care and forethought were exercised; for it was determined to forgo some advantage in punishing the enemy, although all were burning for revenge, rather than to punish him at the cost of any loss to the men.

Caesar sent messengers to the neighboring tribes, holding out to all the hope of plunder and inviting them to harry the Eburones; for Gauls should risk their lives in the forests and not his legionaries, and at the same time to surround the people with a mighty host, and, in requital for their signal villainy, to destroy them, root, branch, and name. Large numbers speedily assembled from every side. While these events were passing in all parts of the Eburonian territory, the last day of the week was approaching, by which time Caesar had determined to return to the legion that guarded his baggage. Now occurred an instance of the power which Fortune wields in war and of the hazards with which Fortune is fraught. The enemy, as we have pointed out, were scattered and panic-stricken, and there was no force to give the slightest ground for alarm. The rumor made its way across the Rhine to the Germans that the Eburones were being harried, and, what was more, that all comers were invited to plunder them. The Sugambri, who dwell in the immediate neighborhood of the Rhine, and who, as we have stated above, sheltered the Tencteri and Usipetes after their flight, raised two thousand horse; crossed the Rhine in barges and on rafts thirty miles below the spot where Caesar had built his bridge and had left a garrison; invaded the nearest part of the Eburonian territory; captured a large number of scattered fugitives; and seized a great quantity of cattle, which uncivilized peoples greatly prize. Lured on by the hope of plunder, they advanced further; and these born warriors and freebooters were not to be stopped by marsh or forest. They asked their prisoners whereabouts Caesar was; found that he had gone far away; and satisfied themselves that his whole army had quitted the neighborhood. Thereupon one of the prisoners asked, "Why go after this wretched, worthless loot when in a twinkling you can make your fortunes? In three hours you can get to Aduatuca, where the Roman army have stored all their belongings: the garrison are a mere handful, unable even to man the wall, and not a soul dares stir out of the entrenchments." Here was a chance. The Germans concealed and left behind the booty they had got, and pushed on for Aduatuca, guided by the man from whom they had learned the news.

Cicero, in obedience to Caesar's instructions, had been most careful to keep his troops every day in camp, not even allowing a single servant to stir outside the entrenchment. On the seventh day, however, hearing more than once that Caesar had advanced to a great distance, and not receiving any intimation of his return, he was afraid that he would not keep his appointment; at the same time he was disquieted by the remarks of the men, who said that, if one mightn't even leave the camp, what he called patience was virtually submission to blockade; and with nine legions and a powerful body of cavalry in the field, and an enemy scattered and all but annihilated, he never expected such a contingency as a disaster within three miles of camp. Accordingly he sent five cohorts to reap the nearest crops, which were only separated from the camp by a solitary hill. Many invalids belonging to the various legions had been left in camp. About three hundred of these, who had recovered in the course of the week, were sent out with the cohorts under a separate command; and a large number of servants got permission to go as well, with a great quantity of baggage cattle which had been stabled in the camp.

Just at this critical moment up came the German horsemen, and, riding right on without slackening speed, tried to break into the camp at the rear gate: woods obstructed the view on that side, and they were not seen till they were getting close to the camp, so that the traders, whose tents were at the foot of the rampart, had no chance of retreating. Our men, being off their guard, were startled by the suddenness of the attack, and the cohort on duty barely withstood the first shock. The enemy spread round the other sides, to see if they could find an entrance. Our men with difficulty defended the gates; but the strength of the position as well as the entrenchments forbade any attempt to enter elsewhere. The whole camp was a scene of confusion, every man asking his neighbour the reason of the uproar; and there was no attempt to determine where the troops should advance or at what point the men were to fall in. One declared that the camp was already taken; another insisted that the natives had come, flushed with victory, from destroying the army and the chief; nearly all, remembering where they were, conceived superstitious fancies and pictured to themselves the disaster that had befallen Cotta and Titurius, who, as they imagined, had perished in the same fort. All being thus panic-stricken, the barbarians were confirmed in the notion, derived from their prisoner, that there was no force within. Striving to break through, they exhorted each other not to let such a chance slip from their grasp.

Publius Sextius Baculus, who had served Bacuius under Caesar's command as principal centurion and who has been mentioned in connection with earlier engagements, had been left invalided in the garrison, and had not tasted food for five days. Feeling anxious for his own safety and that of his comrades, he walked unarmed out of his tent, and, seeing the menacing attitude of the enemy and the extreme peril of the situation, borrowed weapons from the men nearest him and planted himself in the gateway. The centurions of the cohort on guard followed him, and for a short space they sustained the brunt of the fight together. Severely wounded, Sextius fainted and was with difficulty saved by being passed along from hand to hand. The breathing-space thus gained enabled the rest to pluck up courage enough to man the fortifications and make a show of defense.

Meanwhile our soldiers heard the din from afar. The horsemen rode on ahead, and learned the gravity of the danger. There was no entrenchment here to shelter the men in their terror: raw recruits, with no experience of war, they turned to their tribune and centurions, waiting for orders. Not one of them had the courage to keep cool in the face of the unexpected. The barbarians descried the standards in the distance and abandoned their attack. At first they believed that the legions, which, as they had learned from their prisoners, had gone on a distant expedition, had returned; but afterwards, seeing that they were a mere handful, they charged them on every side.

The servants ran forward to a knoll close by. They were speedily dislodged and rushed pell-mell into the maniples as they stood in line, thereby increasing the terror of the soldiers. Some voted for forming in a wedge and making a rapid dash through the enemy, urging that, as the camp was so near, most of them could escape even if a few were cut off and killed; others for standing firm upon the hill and all taking their chance together. The veterans, who, as we have stated, had gone out with the rest under a separate command, disapproved of this suggestion. Accordingly, led by Gains Trebonius, a Roman knight, who had been placed in command of them, they charged, with mutual exhortations, through the midst of the enemy, and reached camp without the loss of a man. The servants and cavalry, following close behind, joined in the charge of the infantry and owed their escape to their courage. Those, however, who had taken their stand upon the hill, and who even now had not learned what fighting meant, could neither abide by their own resolution and defend themselves on their position of vantage, nor imitate the swift energy which, as they saw, was the salvation of the others, but, in their attempt to get back to camp, abandoned the advantage of their position. The centurions, some of whom had been promoted for valour from the lower grades of the other legions to the higher grades of this, determined not to forfeit the credit they had earned in the field, and died fighting with the greatest gallantry. Their brave stand compelling the enemy to fall back, some of the soldiers unexpectedly reached camp in safety; the rest were surrounded by the natives and perished.

The Germans, seeing that our men had by this time manned the works, abandoned the camp and re-crossed the Rhine with the booty which they had left in the woods. Even after they had gone, the panic was so great that Gaius Volusenus, who had been sent on with the cavalry, on arriving in camp that night, could not make the men believe that Caesar was close by and the army with him, safe and sound. Fear had so completely taken possession of them that they were almost beside themselves, and maintained that the whole force must have been annihilated and that the cavalry had alone escaped the rout; for, they insisted, if the army had been safe, the Germans would not have attacked the camp. Caesar's arrival, however, dispelled the panic.

Caesar was well aware that in war it is the unexpected that happens. On his return, therefore, he made no complaint except that the cohorts had been allowed to leave their proper place in the garrison, remarking that no opening should have been left even for the slightest accident; and he considered that Fortune had shown her great power in the enemy's sudden arrival, and still more in having repelled the natives when they had all but gained the rampart and the gates of the camp. The most remarkable point in the whole incident was that the Germans, having crossed the Rhine with the object of ravaging the territories of Ambiorix, had been led to attack the Roman camp, and had thereby done Ambiorix the greatest service that he could desire.

Caesar set out once more to harry the enemy, and, having got together a great horde from the neighboring tribes, let them loose in every direction. Every hamlet, every building that was to be seen was fired; cattle were driven in from all parts; and the corn was not only devoured by the immense multitude of horses and men, but also laid by the autumnal rains. In fact, it seemed certain that even if any of the inhabitants concealed themselves for the time, they must perish, after the withdrawal of the army, from utter destitution. The cavalry, which was very numerous, was sent out in all directions. Often success was all but in their grasp, for prisoners, who had just descried Ambiorix making Escape of off, looked round and insisted that he was barely out of sight; so that his pursuers, seeing a chance of running him down, made herculean efforts and, in the expectation of winning Caesar's favor, showed almost superhuman zeal; but always they seemed just to miss complete success: the quarry broke away from wooded glade or other lair, and, hiding in the night, made for another part of the country. His only escort was four horsemen, to whom alone he ventured to trust his life.

After ravaging the districts in this way, Caesar led back his army, with the loss of two cohorts, to Durocortorum in the country of the Remi, at which place he convened a Gallic council and proceeded to hold an inquiry into the conspiracy of the Senones and Carnutes. He pronounced the extreme sentence on Acco, the author of the movement, and executed him in the time-honored Roman fashion. Some of the conspirators, fearing to be brought to trial, fled and Caesar interdicted them from fire and water. Having quartered two legions for the winter close to the Treveran frontier, two among the Lingones, and the remaining six at Agedincum in the country of the Senones, and arranged for a supply of corn for the army, he set out, according to his custom, for Italy, to hold the assizes.

BOOK VII

The rebellion of Vercingetorix

Gaul was now tranquillized; and Caesar, in accordance with his determination, started for Italy to hold the assizes. There he was informed at
Rome of the murder of Clodius; and, learning that the Senate had decreed
that all Italians eligible for service should be sworn in, he proceeded to levy
troops throughout the whole Province. The news of these events speedily
made its way into Transalpine Gaul. The Gauls amplified and embellished
the story as the facts seemed to warrant, spreading rumors that Caesar was
detained by the disturbances in the capital, and that, while these fierce con-
flicts were raging, he could not rejoin his army. The opportunity stimulated
the Gauls. They were already smarting under their subjection to the Roman
People; and they now began, unreservedly and boldly, to form projects for
war. The leading men of Gaul mutually arranged meetings in secluded
woodland spots. They spoke bitterly of the death of Acco, telling their hear-
ers that the same fate might befall them; and, deploring the fortune that
oppressed the whole country, they made promises and offered rewards of
every kind to induce volunteers to strike the first blow and risk their lives to
restore the liberty of Gaul. The first step was to contrive a plan for cutting
off Caesar from his army before their secret designs could get abroad. This
could be easily done; for the legions would not venture to leave their quarters in the general's absence, and the general would not be able to get to the
legions without an escort. Finally, it was better to die in battle than to fail in
recovering their old military renown and the freedom which was their herit-
age from their forefathers. At the close of the debate the Carnutes declared
that they would shrink from no peril for the common weal, and promised to
strike the first blow; and as, in the circumstances, it was impossible to give
mutual security by exchanging hostages, for fear they should get abroad,
they demanded that the confederates should make a sheaf of their military
standards —an act which, according to Gallic custom, involves a most awful
rite—and bind themselves by solemn oath, as a pledge that, after they had
begun the war, the others should not leave them in the lurch. The Carnutes
were loudly cheered; all who were present took the oath; a date was fixed
for the enterprise; and then the assembly dispersed.

When the appointed day came round and the signal was given, the Carnutes, led by two desperadoes named Cotuatus and Conconnetodumnus, swooped down upon Cenabum; killed the Roman citizens who had settled in the place for trade — amongst others Gaius Cita, a Roman knight of good position, whom Caesar had placed in charge of the commissariat —and plundered their stores. The news spread swiftly to all the tribes of Gaul; for whenever an event of signal importance occurs, the people make it known by loud cries over the countryside, and others in turn take up the cry and pass it on to their neighbors. So it happened on this occasion. The events which had occurred at Cenabum at sunrise were heard of in the country of the Arverni before the close of the first watch, the distance being about one hundred and sixty miles.

In this country dwelt Vercingetorix, son of Celtillus, a young Arvernian of commanding influence, whose father had held the foremost position numerous in all Gaul, and had been put to death by his elected tribe for trying to make himself king. Following the lead of the conspirators, he called his retainers together, and easily inflamed their passions. On learning his design, men flew to arms. Gobannitio, his father's brother, and the other chiefs, who thought that this was no occasion for tempting fortune, frowned upon his enterprise and expelled him from Gergovia: still he did not abandon his purpose, but raised a posse of needy and desperate men in the rural districts. Master of this force, he won over every tribesman whom he approached, and urged them to take up arms in the cause of national freedom; and raising a numerous host, he drove his opponents, by whom he had himself just before been banished, to leave the country. His adherents saluted him as king. He sent out envoys in every direction, adjuring the confederates to remain true. He quickly secured the adhesion of the Senones, Parisii, Pictones, Cadurci, Turoni, Aulerci, Lemovices, Andi, and all the other maritime tribes; and the chief command was conferred upon him unanimously. Armed with this power, he ordered all these tribes to give hostages and bring him speedily a definite quota of troops. He fixed a date by which each tribe was to turn out a specified quantity of arms from its own workshops, and devoted special attention to his cavalry. With the utmost diligence he combined the utmost severity in the exercise of his command, coercing waverers by heavy penalties. Thus he punished serious misdemeanors by death at the stake with all kinds of tortures, while he sent home minor offenders with their ears lopped off or eye gouged out, that they might serve as a warning to the rest and that the severity of their punishment might make others quail.

By these stern measures he speedily raised insurrection. He sent a Cadurcan, named Lucterius, a man of the greatest daring, with a detachment into the country of the Ruteni; while he marched in person for the country of the Bituriges. On his approach the Bituriges sent envoys to the Aedui, whose overlordship they acknowledged, asking for aid to enable them to offer a better resistance to the enemy's force. The Aedui, acting on the advice of the generals whom Caesar had left with the army, sent a force of cavalry and infantry to their assistance. When they reached the Loire—the boundary between the Bituriges and the Aedui—they lingered there a few days, and then turned back without venturing to cross the river. They told the generals that they had returned from fear of treachery on the part of the Bituriges, as they had found out that it was their intention, if they crossed the river, to hem them in on one side, while the Arverni hemmed them in on the other. Whether they acted for the reason which they stated to the generals or from motives of treachery we have no certain knowledge, and therefore do not think it right to make any positive statement. On their departure the Bituriges immediately joined the Arverni.

By the time that news of these events reached Caesar in Italy, he was aware that the situation in the capital had improved, and accordingly started for Transalpine Gaul. On his arrival he found it very difficult to devise a plan for getting to his army. He realized that if he summoned the legions to the Province they would fight a battle on the march without his being present; if, on the other hand, he pushed on alone to join the army, he saw that he could not prudently trust his safety, at such a crisis, even to the tribes which were apparently peaceable.

Meanwhile the Cadurcan, Lucterius, who had been sent into the country of the Ruteni, induced that tribe to join the Arverni. Advancing into the territories of the Nitiobroges and Gabali, he took hostages from both, and, collecting a large force, attempted to make a raid into the Province, in the direction of Narbo. On receiving news of this, Caesar deemed it imperative, before doing anything else, to march for Narbo. Arriving there, he encouraged the faint-hearted detachments among the Provincial Ruteni, the Volcae Arecomici, the Tolosates, and in the districts round Narbo which were in proximity to the enemy, and ordered a part of the Provincial troops and a fresh draft which he had brought from Italy to concentrate in the country of the Helvii, which is conterminous with that of the Arverni.

As a result of these measures, Lucterius was checked and in fact forced to retire, for he thought it hazardous to venture within the chain of posts; and accordingly Caesar started for the country of the Helvii. It was the most rigorous season of the year, and the Cevennes, which separates the Arverni from the Helvii, was covered by snow of extraordinary depth, which made marching difficult; but the snow, which was six feet deep, was shoveled aside, and, the roads being thus cleared by prodigious exertion on the part of the men, he made his way to the country of the Arverni. They were taken completely by surprise, for they had always supposed that the Cevennes protected them like a wall, and at that time of the year the tracks had never been practicable even for solitary travelers. Caesar ordered his cavalry to scour the country far and wide, and do their utmost to strike terror into the enemy. The news travelled swiftly by rumor and dispatches to Vercingetorix; and the Arverni in great alarm all thronged round him and besought him to have some consideration for them and not let them be pillaged by the enemy, for he must see that the whole brunt of the war had been shifted on to them. Yielding to their entreaties, he moved from the country of the Bituriges towards that of the Arverni.

Caesar had anticipated that this would happen with Vercingetorix; therefore, after remaining a couple of days in the district, he left the army on the pretext of having to concentrate the new draft and the cavalry, and placed the younger Brutus in command of the troops, charging him to make the cavalry scour the country in all directions, far and wide, and announcing that he would do his best not to stay away from camp more than three days. Having settled these matters, he made his way, as fast as he could possibly travel, to Vienna, before his troops expected him; picked up his cavalry there, which he had sent on a considerable time before, in good condition; and pushed on through the country of the Aedui, marching night and day, so that in case they had any intention of molesting him he might be too quick for them, till he reached the country of the Lingones, where two legions were wintering. On his arrival he sent word to the remaining legions, and concentrated them all before news of his arrival could reach the Arverni. Vercingetorix, on hearing what he had done, led his army back into the country of the Bituriges, and moving thence, proceeded to besiege Gorgobina, a stronghold of the Boii, whom Caesar had established there after their defeat in the battle with the Helvetii, and had placed in dependence on the Aedui.

Caesar was greatly embarrassed by this move. If he kept his legions concentrated for the rest of the winter, and the tributaries of the Aedui were overpowered, the whole of Gaul, seeing that he could not be relied upon to protect his friends, might simultaneously fall away: if, on the other hand, he prematurely withdrew the army from its quarters, he might be pressed for supplies owing to the difficulties of transport. Still, it seemed better to face every difficulty than to alienate all who were on his side by submitting to an indignity like this. Accordingly he charged the Aedui to forward supplies, and sent on messengers to let the Boii know that he was coming and to urge them to remain faithful and sustain the enemy's attack with fortitude. Then, leaving two legions and the heavy baggage of the whole army at Agedincum, he set out to join the Boii.

Next day he reached Vellaunodunum, a stronghold of the Senones. In order to avoid leaving an enemy in his rear and so expedite supply, he proceeded to besiege the town, and in a couple of days surrounded it. On the third day envoys were sent out to propose surrender. Caesar ordered the garrison to pile arms, bring out their horses, and give six hundred hostages. He left Gaius Trebonius to give effect to these orders, and, being anxious to finish his march as soon as possible, pushed on for Cenabum in the country of the Carnutes. Believing that the siege of Vellaunodunum, news of which had only just reached them, would be protracted, they were beginning to collect troops to send to the protection of Cenabum. Caesar reached the town in a couple of days. He encamped before it; but, as recaptures it was late in the day and he was prevented from beginning the siege, he postponed it till the morrow, ordering the troops to make all needful preparations; and, as there was a bridge over the Loire in contact with the town and he feared that the garrison might escape in the night, he directed two legions to remain under arms. Shortly before midnight the townspeople moved silently out of Cenabum and began to cross the river. The movement was reported to Caesar by his patrols, whereupon he fired the gates, sent in the legions which he had ordered to remain in readiness, and took possession of the town. Very few of the enemy escaped capture; for the narrowness of the bridge and streets prevented the throng from getting away. Caesar plundered and burned the town; gave the booty to the soldiers; threw his army across the Loire, and made his way into the country of the Bituriges.

When Vercingetorix learned that Caesar and captures was approaching, he abandoned the siege and marched to encounter him. Caesar had prepared to besiege a stronghold of the Bituriges, called Noviodunum, situated upon his line of march. Envoys came from the town to beg him to pardon them and to spare their lives; and, in order to finish the campaign as rapidly as he had begun it, he ordered the garrison to pile their arms, bring out their horses, and give hostages. Some of the hostages had been delivered up and the other arrangements were in progress, the centurions and a few soldiers having been sent into the town to collect the arms and cattle, when the enemy's cavalry, which had gone on in advance of Vercingetorix's column, were seen in the distance. The moment the townspeople caught sight of them, they realized that there was a chance of relief; and with a yell they seized their arms, shut the gates,, and manned the walls. The centurions in the town, understanding from the behavior of the Gauls that they meant mischief, drew their swords, took possession of the gates, and withdrew all their men in safety.

Caesar ordered his cavalry out of camp, and forced on an engagement: presently, his men being in difficulties, he sent about four hundred German horse, whom he had regularly entertained from the first, to the rescue. The Gauls, unable to sustain their charge, were put to flight, and fell back, with heavy loss, upon the main body. On their defeat, the townsmen again took alarm, and, seizing the individuals whom they believed to have been instrumental in stirring up the rabble, took them to Caesar and surrendered. This affair disposed of, Caesar marched for Avaricum, the largest and strongest town in the against country of the Bituriges, which is situated in a very fertile tract, for he was confident that by the recovery of this stronghold he would re-establish his authority over the tribe.

Having sustained these successive disasters, at Vellaunodunum, Cenabum, and Noviodunum, Vercingetorix called his followers to a council, and ordered them that the campaign must thence forward be conducted on widely different lines. The object was by every means to prevent the Romans from foraging and getting supplies. This object could easily be attained; for their side was strong in cavalry, and the season was in their favor. No grass could be cut; the enemy must perforce disperse and get fodder from the barns; and the cavalry could destroy all these detachments from day to day. Moreover, in the public interest, personal convenience must be disregarded: all round the road, as far as the country was accessible for forage, the hamlets and homesteads should be burned. They were well off for supplies themselves, as they could draw upon the resources of the people whose territory was the theatre of the war: but the Romans would either succumb to their privations or would have to move far from their camp at great risk; and it made no difference whether they killed them or took their baggage, for, if it were lost, they could not keep the field. Moreover, it would be well to burn those towns which were not rendered impregnable by fortification and a naturally strong position, for fear they should serve their own side as refuges for shirking military duty, and tempt the Romans to pillage them and plunder their stores. If this sounded hard or cruel, they should consider how much harder it was for their wives and children to be carried off into slavery while they were themselves put to death; and if they were beaten, this would be inevitable.

This view was unanimously approved; and in a single day more than twenty towns belonging to the Bituriges were set ablaze. The same thing happened in the territories of the other tribes: the whole country was a scene of conflagration; and although all felt this a grievous trial, they consoled themselves with the assurance that victory was practically in their grasp and that they would soon recover what they had lost. The question was debated in a general assembly, whether Avaricum should be burned or defended. The Bituriges knelt before their countrymen, begging that they might not be forced to fire with their own hands the town which was well-nigh the finest in the whole of Gaul,—the bulwark and the pride of their people: it was naturally so strong that they would easily defend it; for it was almost entirely surrounded by running water and marshy ground, and could only be approached at one place, which was very narrow. Their prayer was granted. Vercingetorix at first opposed them, but afterwards gave way, in deference to their entreaties and the general sympathy that was shown them. Capable officers were selected to defend the town.

Vercingetorix, following Caesar, selected for his encampment a spot, protected by marshes and woods, sixteen miles from Avaricum. He hourly kept himself informed, by organized patrols, of what was going on at Avaricum, and issued his orders accordingly. He watched all our expeditions for forage and corn, attacked our men when they were scattered—for they were obliged to go far afield—and inflicted on them considerable loss, although they took every precaution that ingenuity could devise to baffle him, starting at odd times and in different directions.

Caesar encamped on the side of the town siege of which, as we have mentioned above, was undefended by running water and marshy ground, and was approached by a narrow neck of land. As the lie of the country made it impossible to invest the position, he proceeded to build a terrace, form lines of sheds, and erect two towers. He urged the Boii and the Aedui unceasingly to keep him supplied with grain: but the latter, being halfhearted, were of little service; while the former, a small and feeble tribe, whose resources were slender, soon used up what they had. Owing to the poverty of the Boii, the slackness of the Aedui, and the burning of the granaries, the army was in the greatest straits for supplies, insomuch that for several days the men were without grain, and only kept famine at bay by driving in the cattle from distant villages: yet not a word were they heard to utter unworthy of the majesty of the Roman People and their own record of victory. Nor was this all. Caesar spoke to the legions singly while they were at work, and told them that, if they found their privations too hard to bear, he would abandon the siege; but with one voice they begged him not to do so: they had served under his command for several years without disgrace, and had never abandoned any operation which they had undertaken. They would feel it a disgrace to abandon the siege, having once begun it; and it was better to put up with every hardship than fail in avenging the Romans who had fallen at Cenabum by Gallic treachery. They said the same to the centurions and tribunes, charging them to repeat it to Caesar.

The towers were now getting close to the wall. Caesar learned from prisoners that Vercingetorix, having consumed his provender, had moved closer to Avaricum, and gone off himself with his cavalry and the light-armed foot who regularly fight along with the cavalry, intending to lie in ambush at the spot where he believed that our men would go to forage on the following day. Acting on this information, Caesar started quietly at midnight and reached the enemy's encampment in the morning. They were informed of his approach by their patrols, and, swiftly removing their carts and baggage into the densest parts of the woods, drew up all their forces on open rising ground. On receiving this report Caesar ordered the troops to pile their packs promptly and get their arms ready.

The hill sloped gently upward from its base, and was almost entirely surrounded by marshy ground, difficult to cross, but not more than fifty feet wide. The Gauls had broken down the causeways and remained obstinately on the hill, confident in the strength of the position; formed up in tribal groups, they held all the fords and the thickets that bordered the marsh, determined, if the Romans attempted to force a passage, to attack them from their commanding position while they were bogged in the slush. Seeing the proximity of the two forces, one would have thought that the Gauls were ready to fight and that the chances were nearly even; but anyone who detected the disparity in the conditions would have known that their defiant attitude was mere bravado. The legionaries, indignant that the enemy behind that paltry barrier had the hardihood to look them in the face, clamored for the signal for action: but Caesar made them understand that victory could only be gained at a heavy cost and by the sacrifice of many brave men; he could see that for his honor their hearts were steeled to face any peril, and for that reason he should deserve to be called the most heartless of men if he did not hold their lives dearer than his own reputation. In this way he soothed the men's feelings, and, leading them back the same day to camp, proceeded to complete his arrangements for the siege of the town.

Vercingetorix, on returning to his troops, was accused of treachery. The charge was that he had moved nearer the Romans; that he had taken all the cavalry with him; that he had left his numerous forces without a head; and that on his departure the Romans had rapidly advanced at the opportune moment. These things could not all have happened by accident: they must have been deliberately planned; and evidently he would rather reign over Gaul as Caesar's creature than by the favor of his countrymen. In reply to these charges Vercingetorix said that if he had shifted his camp, he had done so because forage was scarce and at their own instigation; if he had moved nearer to the Romans, it was because he was attracted by a favourable position, whose natural features were its own defense; while cavalry ought not to have been required on marshy ground, and were useful in the place to which they had actually gone. When he left them he had deliberately refrained from delegating the command to any one, for fear his substitute might be driven by the impetuosity of the host to fight; for he could see that that was what they all wanted, because they were infirm of purpose and incapable of prolonged exertion. If the arrival of the Romans in his absence was accidental, they ought to thank Fortune; if they had come on the invitation of a spy, they ought to thank him for having enabled them to ascertain from their commanding position the smallness of their numbers, and to see how despicable was the spirit of men who dared not fight, but slunk back ignominiously to their camp. For himself, he did not want to get from Caesar by treachery a power which he could secure by victory,—victory which was already in his grasp and in that of the whole Gallic people. No! he would give them back their gift if they imagined that they were conferring a favor upon him instead of owing their safety to him.

"To satisfy yourselves," he continued, "that what I say is true, listen to Roman soldiers!"

He made some slaves step forward, whom he had captured foraging a few days before, and had kept in chains on starvation diet. They had been carefully taught beforehand what to say when questioned. They said that they were legionaries: hunger and want had led them to steal out of camp to see whether they could find any corn or cattle in the fields; the whole army was in the same straits, and not a man was now strong enough to stand the strain of his daily work. The General had therefore resolved to withdraw the army in three days unless he made some real progress in the siege of the town.

"These benefits," said Vercingetorix, "you owe to me,—me, whom you falsely accuse of treachery: thanks to my efforts, without shedding a drop of your blood you see this mighty, this victorious army well-nigh starved; and I have taken care that, when it seeks safety in ignominious flight, not one tribe shall grant it refuge."

The whole multitude cheered loudly and receive clashed their weapons in the native fashion; for acclamation. Gauls generally do this when they are pleased with what an orator says. Vercingetorix, they declared, was the greatest of leaders: his loyalty was above suspicion; and it was impossible to carry on the war with greater judgement They determined to throw ten thousand men, selected from all the contingents, into the town, not thinking it wise to trust the national safety to the Bituriges alone; for they realized that if the Bituriges succeeded in holding the town, the whole victory would be theirs.

The extraordinary valour of our soldiers found its match in the manifold devices of the Gauls; for they are a most ingenious people, and always show the greatest aptitude in borrowing and giving effect to ideas which they get from any one. They pulled aside the grappling-hooks with nooses, and when they had got hold of them hauled them inside the town by means of windlasses. They also undermined and dragged away the material of the terrace, performing the operation very adroitly, because there are large iron-mines in their country, and they are thoroughly familiar with every kind of underground gallery. Moreover, they had covered the whole wall at every point with towers, provided with platforms, and protected by hides. Again, they made frequent sorties by day and night, setting fire to the terrace or attacking the troops at their work: as the terrace, daily rising, raised our tow-ers to a higher level, they lashed together the uprights of their own towers, and gave them a corresponding elevation; and opening into the Roman mines, they prevented them, with beams sharpened and hardened in the fire, boiling pitch, and heavy stones, from approaching the wall.

Gallic walls are always constructed on the following or some similar plan. Balks of timber are laid upon the ground, at right angles to the line of the intended wall and in unbroken succession along its length, at regular intervals of two feet. These balks are made fast on the inner side and thickly coated with rubble; while the intervals above mentioned are tightly packed in front with large stones. When the balks are fixed in their places and fas-tened together, a fresh row is laid on the top of them in such a way that the same interval is kept, and the balks do not touch each other, but are separat-ed by similar intervals, into each of which a stone is thrust, and thus are kept firmly in position. Thus, step by step, the whole fabric is constructed until the wall reaches its proper height. While the structure, with its alternate balks and stones, which preserve their regular succession in straight lines, presents a variegated aspect which is not unsightly, it is also extremely ser-viceable and adapted for the defense of towns; for the stone secures it against fire, and the woodwork, which is braced on the inner side by beams generally forty feet long running right across, and so can neither be broken through nor pulled to pieces, protects it against the ram.

All the above-mentioned causes impeded the siege, and the men were hampered all the time by cold and continual rain; yet by unremitting toil they overcame all these difficulties, and in twenty-five days erected a terrace three hundred and thirty feet broad and eighty feet high. The terrace was almost in contact with the enemy's wall, and Caesar was, as usual, bivouack-ing at the works, urging the men not to suspend labour for a moment, when, a little before the third watch, it was noticed that the terrace was smoking. The enemy had undermined and set it on fire. At the same moment a cheer arose all along the wall and troops came pouring out of the two gates on ei-ther side of the towers, while others flung down torches and dry wood from their commanding position on the wall on to the terrace, and shot pitch and other inflammable material; so that it was scarcely possible to decide where to strike a counter blow or what point to reinforce. But Caesar's practice was to have two legions regularly bivouacking in front of the camp, while a larger number, which took duty in turns, were constantly at work; so that a number of men soon checked the sortie, while others drew back the towers and dragged asunder the timbers of the terrace, and the whole multitude from the camp came thronging to extinguish the flames.

The rest of the night passed by; and still the fight was going on at every point. The enemy's hope of victory continually revived, for they saw that the breastworks of the towers were burnt, and that it was not easy to advance and support a threatened position without cover; in their own ranks fresh men were continually relieving those who were tired, and they felt that on that moment depended the salvation of Gaul:—just then we witnessed an episode which seemed worthy of remembrance and we have therefore thought ought not to be passed over. A Gaul, standing in front of one of the gates of the town, was throwing lumps of fat and pitch, passed to him from hand to hand, into the fire opposite one of the towers. A bolt from a small catapult pierced him on the right side, and he dropped dead. One of the men nearest him stepped across his prostrate body and continued the work; a shot from the catapult killed him in the same way, and a third man took his place, and a fourth the place of the third; nor was the post abandoned by the defenders until the fire on the terrace was put out, the enemy everywhere repulsed, and the fighting at an end.

The Gauls had tried every expedient; and next day, as nothing had succeeded, they took the urgent advice of Vercingetorix and determined to escape from the town. By making the attempt in the stillness of night they hoped to succeed without much loss; for Vercingetorix's camp was not far from the town, and the continuous marsh which intervened would make it difficult for the Romans to pursue. It was night and they were preparing for their attempt, when suddenly the matrons came running into the open and, weeping and flinging themselves at their husbands' feet, passionately entreated them not to give them up and the children who were their common possession to the tender mercies of the enemy; for natural bodily weakness prevented them from making their escape. When they saw that their resolve was immovable—for often in extremity of peril fear leaves no room for compassion—they began to scream and gesticulate, to warn the Romans of the intended flight. The Gauls were terrified by this, fearing that the Roman cavalry would seize the roads, and abandoned their resolve.

Next day, Caesar advanced one of his towers; and the works which he had begun were completed. A heavy storm of rain came on, and he thought the opportunity a good one for maturing his plans. Observing that the guards were rather carelessly posted on the wall, he ordered his own men to go about their work with a show of listlessness, and explained his intention.

The legions, unobserved, got ready for action under the cover of the sheds. Caesar told them that now was the moment to repay themselves for their herculean toils and grasp the prize of victory; and, offering rewards to the men who should first mount the wall, he gave the troops the signal. Suddenly they darted forth from every point and swiftly lined the wall.

The enemy, panic-stricken by this unexpected move, were driven from the wall and towers, but formed in wedge-shaped masses in the market-place and open spaces, determined, if they were attacked, to fight it out, shoulder to shoulder. Seeing that no one would come down on to the level, but that men were swarming all along the wall on every side, they feared that all chance of escape would be gone, and, flinging away their arms, made a rush for the furthest quarter of the town. There some of them, jostling one another in the narrow gateways, were slaughtered by the infantry, and others, after they had got clear of the gates, by the cavalry. Not a man reeked of plunder. Exasperated by the massacre at Cenabum and the toil of the siege, they spared not the aged, nor women, nor children. Of the entire garrison, numbering about forty thousand, a bare eight hundred, who had fled precipitately from the town on hearing the first outcry, escaped unhurt to Vercingetorix. Late at night he received the fugitives in silence. Fearing that, as they came thronging in, the sympathies of the host might be aroused and a riot ensue in the camp, he stationed his trusted associates and the tribal leaders some distance off on the road, and had the fugitives conveyed separately to join their comrades in the sections of the camp which had been allotted originally to each tribe.

Next day he called a council of war and consoled his followers, bidding them not be unduly disheartened or disquieted by the disaster. Romans had not beaten them by superior courage or in fair fight, but by a kind of trickery and by their knowledge of siege-work, of which they themselves had no experience. It was a mistake to expect invariable success in war. They could testify that he had never approved of defending Avaricum: this reverse was due to the short-sightedness of the Bituriges and the undue complaisance of the other tribes. However, he would soon repair it by successes greater still. By good management he would gain over the dissentient tribes and make the whole of Gaul of one mind; and when Gaul was united, the whole world could not stand against her. This object, indeed, he had already nearly attained. Meanwhile he had a right to expect, in the name of the common weal, that they would take to fortifying their camps, so as to withstand sudden attacks more readily.

This speech made a good impression upon the Gauls. What pleased them most was that, despite a signal disaster, Vercingetorix had not lost heart or concealed himself or shrunk from facing the multitude; and they gave him all the more credit for foresight and prescience because, before the event, he had voted, first for the burning of Avaricum and afterwards for its abandonment. And so, while a reverse weakens the authority of commanders in general, his prestige, on the contrary, in consequence of the disaster, waxed daily greater. At the same time, relying upon his assurance, they entertained the hope of gaining over the other tribes. Gauls now for the first time began to fortify their camps; and they were so thoroughly frightened that, unused though they were to labour, they felt constrained to submit to every order.

Vercingetorix was as good as his word, and exercised his ingenuity to gain over the other tribes, tempting their chiefs by presents and offers of reward. He chose agents qualified for the purpose, selecting them for the persuasive power which they could exercise by plausible speech or good-fellowship. He made it his business to provide those who had escaped on the fall of Avaricum with arms and clothing; at the same time, in order to make good his losses, he levied a definite number of recruits from the tribes, fixing the strength of each contingent and the date by which he required them to arrive at headquarters; and he gave orders that all the archers in Gaul—a very numerous body—should be searched for and sent to him. By these measures the losses at Avaricum were speedily repaired. Meanwhile Teutomatus, king of the Nitiobroges, whose father had received from our Senate the title of Friend, joined him with a large body of his own cavalry and of others from Aquitania whom he had hired.

Caesar remained several days at Avaricum, where he found an abundance of grain and other stores, and thus enabled the army to recover from their labour and privation. Winter was now nearly over: the propitious season bade him take the field; and he had determined to march against the enemy in the hope of being able to lure him out of the marshes and forests or to keep him under close blockade, when the Aeduan magnates came as envoys to beg him to help their country in a serious emergency. The situation, they pleaded, was extremely critical. From remote antiquity the chief magistrates had regularly been appointed one at a time and held sovereign power for one year; now, however, there were two in office, each of whom asserted that his appointment was legal. One of them was Convictolitavis, a young man of influence and distinction; the other Cotus, a scion of a very old family, and, moreover, a man of commanding position and powerful family connections, whose brother, Valetiacus, had held the same office in the preceding year. The people were all up in arms: the council and the commonalty were divided; and the rivals were each supported by their own retainers. If the dispute were prolonged, the result would be civil war. It rested with Caesar to prevent this by his energy and influence.

Caesar considered it detrimental to leave the theatre of war and suspend his operations against the enemy; but he was aware that great disasters commonly arise from civil strife. The Aedui were a powerful tribe, bound by the closest ties to the Roman People: he had always promoted their interests and distinguished them by every mark of favor; and he regarded it as his first duty to prevent them from coming to blows, and the weaker party from applying for aid to Vercingetorix. As the holder of the chief magistracy was forbidden by Aeduan law to leave the country, he determined, in order to avoid the semblance of slighting their rights or their laws, to go in person to their country, and accordingly summoned the whole council and the disputants themselves to meet him at Decetia. There almost all the citizens of note assembled. Caesar was informed that a few persons had been secretly called together, and that one of the rivals had been declared elected by his own brother, in a wrong place and at a wrong time; whereas the law not only forbade two members of one family to be appointed while both were alive, but actually prohibited them from sitting in the council. He therefore compelled Cotus to resign, and authorized Convictolitavis, who had been appointed by the priests, in accordance with tribal custom in a period of interregnum, to continue to hold office.

Having stopped the dispute by this decision, Caesar counselled the Aedui to forget their disputes and dissensions, and, putting aside everything else, to devote themselves to the campaign, and look forward to receiving from him the reward which would be their due when Gaul was finally conquered: they were to send him quickly the whole of their cavalry and ten thousand foot, that he might distribute them for the protection of his convoys. He then divided the army into two parts. Assigning part of the cavalry to Labienus and retaining the rest, he gave him four legions, with which he was to march against the Senones and the Parisii, and advanced in person at the head of the remaining six towards the country of the Arverni, in the direction of the stronghold of Gergovia, following the bridges over the river, and marched up the opposite bank. The two armies were in full view of one another, and each encamped almost parallel with the camp of the other: patrols were thrown out to prevent the Romans from making a bridge anywhere and throwing their troops across; and thus Caesar was in a very difficult position, for he was in danger of being barred by the river for the greater part of the summer, as the Allier is not generally fordable before the autumn. To prevent this, he encamped in a wooded spot opposite which Vercingetorix had broken down, and next day remained there in concealment with two legions; the rest of the force he sent on as usual with all the baggage, breaking up some of the cohorts, so that the number of the legions might appear unchanged. He ordered them to march on as far as possible;

and when he inferred from the time of day that they had reached camp, he proceeded to repair the bridge, making use of the original piles, the lower part of which was still entire. The work was rapidly finished; the legions crossed over; and, selecting a suitable spot for his camp, he recalled the other troops. When Vercingetorix found out what had happened, he pushed on ahead by forced marches, in order to avoid being compelled to fight against his will.

From the point where he had halted Caesar made his way to Gergovia in five marches. On the day of his arrival a cavalry skirmish took place. The town, situated upon a lofty hill, was difficult of access on all sides. After making a reconnaissance, Caesar concluded that a regular siege would be hopeless; and he resolved not to attempt a blockade until he had secured his supplies. Vercingetorix had encamped near the town and grouped the contingents of the several tribes at moderate distances from one another and round his own quarters. His force occupied all the high points of the mountain mass commanding a view over the plain, and presented a formidable appearance. He ordered the tribal chieftains, whom he had chosen to share his counsels, to come to him every morning at daybreak, to communicate intelligence or make arrangements for the defense; and there was hardly a day on which he missed sending his cavalry into action with archers scattered among their ranks, so as to test the mettle and the soldierly qualities of every man. Opposite the town, and at the very foot of the mountain, there was a hill of great natural strength and scarped on every side. If our troops could occupy it, they would probably be able to cut off the enemy from a principal source of their water-supply and harass their foragers; but they held the place, though with an inadequate force. Notwithstanding, Caesar moved out of his camp in the stillness of night, and before relief could arrive from the town, expelled the garrison, took possession of the place, and posted two legions to hold it. From the larger camp to the smaller he drew a pair of trenches, each twelve feet broad, to enable the men to come and go, even one at a time, secure from any sudden attack.

While these events were passing at Gergovia, Convictolitavis, the Aeduan, upon whom, as we have related, Caesar had conferred the chief magistracy, was bribed by the Arverni to join them. He communicated with a number of young men, the most prominent of whom were Litaviccus and his brothers, who belonged to a very illustrious family. Sharing the money with them, he urged them to bear in mind that they were free men, born to command. The Aedui, and they alone, prevented Gaul from making sure of success: their influence kept the other tribes in check; and if it were thrown into the opposite scale, the Romans would have no footing in Gaul. Personally, he was under some obligation to Caesar, though he had fully deserved to win his case; but obligation was outweighed by regard for the national liberty. Why, indeed, should the Aedui submit their rights and laws to the arbitration of Caesar any more than the Romans to that of the Aedui? The young men were speedily won by the magistrate's eloquence and his gold, and promised even to take the lead in his enterprise; and they tried to think of some method of accomplishing it, feeling doubtful whether the community could be lightly induced to embark on war. It was decided that Litaviccus should take command of the ten thousand who were to be sent to Caesar to take part in the campaign, and undertake the duty of leading them, and that his brothers should hurry on in advance to join Caesar. At the same time they arranged the rest of their program.

Litaviccus took command of the army. About thirty miles from Gergovia he suddenly paraded the troops.

"Soldiers," he said, with a burst of tears, "All our cavalry, all our men of rank have perished. Two of our leading citizens, Eporedorix and Aeduan Viridomarus, have been falsely charged with treason and put to death by the Romans without trial. Learn the facts from these men, who have fled straight from the massacre; for my brothers and all my kinsfolk are slain, and grief prevents me from telling what has happened."

Some men whom he had schooled in their parts came forward, and repeated to the host the tale which Litaviccus had told. All the Aeduan cavalry, they said, had been massacred on the rumor that they had been in communication with the Arverni; they had themselves hidden in the crowd of soldiers and escaped from the midst of the slaughter. With one voice the Aedui adjured Litaviccus to consider their safety.

"As if," he cried, "it were a case for consideration! As if we were not bound to hurry on to Gergovia and join the Arverni! Can we doubt that the Romans, after the shameful deed they have done, are even now hastening to slay us? Therefore, if we have a spark of courage in us, let us avenge the deaths of our countrymen who have been most foully murdered, and kill these brigands."

Then, pointing to some Roman citizens who had accompanied him in reliance upon his escort, he seized a quantity of corn and other stores belonging to them, cruelly tortured them, and put them to death. Sending messengers throughout the length and breadth of the Aeduan territory, he stirred up the populace by the same lying tale of the massacre of cavalry and chiefs, and urged them to follow his example and avenge their wrongs.

Eporedorix, a young Aeduan of noble birth and commanding influence in his own country, and Viridomarus, a man of the same age and equally popular, but of lower birth, had been summoned expressly by Caesar, and had taken the field with the cavalry. Diviciacus had recommended Viridomarus to Caesar; and Caesar had raised him from a humble position to the highest dignity. He and Eporedorix were rivals for power; and in the struggle between the magistrates Eporedorix had been a strong partisan of Convictolitavis, and Viridomarus of Cotus. On learning Litaviccus's design, Eporedorix went to Caesar about midnight and told him the story. He begged him not to suffer the tribe to fall away from its friendship with the Roman People through the misguided counsels of raw youths; telling him that he foresaw that this would happen if such a numerous force joined the enemy, for their kinsmen could not disregard their safety or the tribe treat it as insignificant.

The news caused Caesar great anxiety; for he had always shown especial favor to the Aeduan community. Without a moment's hesitation, therefore, he left camp at the head of four legions in light marching order and the whole of the cavalry. There was no time at such a crisis to reduce the size of the camp, for success plainly depended upon prompt action; and he left Gaius Gergovia. Fabius to guard it with two legions. He ordered Litaviccus's brothers to be arrested, but found that they had escaped to the enemy a short time before. Addressing the men, he urged them not to mind a hard march at so critical a conjuncture. They were all in great heart; and, after a march of twenty-five miles, Caesar descried the Aeduan column, and, sending on his cavalry, delayed and finally stopped their advance, at the same time strictly forbidding all ranks to kill a single man, and telling Eporedorix and Viridomarus, who were supposed by the Aedui to have been killed, to move about among the troopers and speak to their countrymen. As soon as they were recognized and the Aedui saw that Litaviccus had deceived them, they stretched out their hands in token of surrender, grounding their arms and begging for their lives. Litaviccus escaped to Gergovia, accompanied by his retainers; for Gallic custom brands it as shameful for retainers to desert their lords even when all is lost.

Caesar sent messengers to the Aedui to explain that, as an act of favor, he had spared men whom the rights of war would have entitled him to put to death; and, after giving the army three hours in the night to rest, he moved on towards Gergovia. About half-way, some horsemen, sent by Fabius, met him and reported that the camp had been in imminent danger. The entire force of the enemy, they said, had attacked it, fresh men frequently relieving their comrades when they were tired, and wearing out our troops by incessant toil, as, on account of its great extent, they had to keep constantly on the rampart without relief Many had been wounded by showers of arrows and missiles of every kind; but the artillery had been of great use in enabling them to hold out. When the enemy retired, Fabius was blocking up all the gates except two, strengthening the rampart with breastworks, and preparing to meet a similar attack on the morrow. On receiving this intelligence, Caesar pushed on, and, thanks to the extraordinary energy of the men, reached camp before sunrise.

While these events were passing at Gergovia, the Aedui received Litaviccus's first message. Leaving themselves no time to find out the truth, they were impelled, some by greed, others by anger and rashness—an innate quality of the race —to take an idle rumor for an ascertained fact. They plundered Roman citizens; murdered them; kidnapped and enslaved them. Convictolitavis added fuel to the flame, and hounded on the masses to frenzy, in the hope that, once committed, they would feel ashamed to return to reason. Marcus Aristius, a military tribune, was on his way to join his legion. They promised him a safe conduct, and made him quit the town of Cabillonum, compelling the Romans who had settled there for trade to depart also. Forthwith they fell upon them on the road and robbed them of all their baggage. The Romans resisted, and their assailants beset them all day and the following night. Many were killed on both sides; and the assailants roused numbers to arm.

Meanwhile news arrived that all their infantry were in Caesar's power. Hurrying to Aristius, they explained that the government was not responsible for anything; and ordering an inquiry about the plundered property, they confiscated the goods of Litaviccus and his brothers, and sent envoys to make their excuses to Caesar. Their motive was to get their countrymen restored; but, stained with crime, fascinated by the profits of plunder (for many had had a hand in the outrages), and dreading retribution, they began to make secret preparations for war, and sent embassies to gain over the other tribes. Caesar was aware of their designs; nevertheless he spoke to their envoys with all possible gentleness, assuring them that he would not judge the whole people harshly because of the ignorant folly of the masses, or abate his goodwill towards the Aedui. Anxiety that the insurrection in Gaul would spread, and desiring to avoid being surrounded by all the tribes, he began to think out a plan for withdrawing from the neighborhood of Gergovia and once more concentrating the whole army in such a way that his departure might not be attributed to fear of a general defection and resemble a flight.

While he was meditating on this problem, he thought he saw an opportunity of striking a telling blow. Going to the smaller camp to inspect the works, he noticed that a hill in the possession of the enemy was completely deserted whereas before it could hardly be discerned for their number. In astonishment, he inquired of the deserters, who daily flocked to join him in great numbers, what was the reason. They were all agreed—and Caesar had already found out the same thing for himself through his patrols—that the ridge to which the hill belonged was nearly level, but where it gave access to the further side of the town wooded and narrow. The Gauls were intensely anxious for the safety of this place; and, one hill being already held by the Romans, they now felt sure that, if they lost the other, they would be all but surrounded, fairly cut off from all egress, and prevented from foraging. Every man, therefore, had been called away by Vercingetorix to fortify the position.

On learning this, Caesar sent several squadrons of cavalry thither about midnight, ordering them to rove all over the country and make a good deal of noise. At daybreak he ordered a large number of pack-horses and mules to be taken out of camp, the pack-saddles to be taken off, and the drivers to put on helmets, so as to look like troopers, and ride round over the hills. He sent a few regular cavalry with them, with orders to wander further afield, so as to increase the effect. All were to make a wide circuit and head towards the same goal. These movements could be seen, far off, from the town, as Gergovia commanded a view of the camp; but it was impossible, at such a distance, to make out exactly what they mean. A single legion was sent along the same chain; and after it had advanced a little way it was stationed on lower ground and concealed in the woods. The suspicions of the Gauls were intensified; and they transferred all their forces to the threatened point to help in the work of fortification. Noticing that the enemy's camps were deserted, Caesar made his soldiers cover their crests and hide their standards, and move, a few at a time, to avoid being observed from the town, from the larger to the smaller camp. At the same time he explained his plans to his generals, each of whom he had placed in command of a legion, warning them above all to keep the men in hand, and not let them advance too far from over-eagerness for fighting or lust for plunder. He pointed out that the unfavorable ground placed them at a disadvantage, which could only be avoided by moving quickly; it was a case for a surprise, not a regular battle. Having made these instructions clear, he gave the signal, at the same time sending the Aedui up the hill by another path on the right.

The wall of the town was nine furlongs in a straight line from the plain, where the ascent began, without reckoning any bend; the turns that were necessary for easing the slope added outer line of so much to the length of the climb. About halfway up, running lengthways in the direction indicated by the formation of the mountain, the Gauls had built a wall six feet high, of large stones, to check any attack by our men. All the space below was left unoccupied; but the higher part of the hill up to the wall of the town was thickly covered by their camps. When the signal was given, the men rapidly gained the outer line of defense, clambered over it, and took possession of three camps. They did this so quickly that Teutomatus, king of the Nitiobroges, was surprised in his tent, where he was taking his siesta, and only just broke away, naked to the waist and with his horse wounded, from the clutches of the plundering soldiers. Having achieved his purpose, Caesar ordered the recall to be sounded, and immediately halted the legion, which he commanded in person. The men of the other legions did not hear the sound of the trumpet, as a considerable valley intervened; still the tribunes and the generals, in obedience to Caesar's command, tried to keep them in hand. Elated, however, by the expectation of a speedy triumph, by the enemy's flight, and by the recollection of past victories, they fancied that nothing was too difficult for their valour to achieve, and pressed on in pursuit till they got close to the wall and gates of the fortress. Then a cry arose from every part of the town; and those who were some way off, panic-stricken by the sudden uproar, and believing that the enemy were inside the gates, rushed pell-mell out of the stronghold. Matrons flung down clothes and money from the wall, and, leaning over with breasts bare, stretched forth their hands and besought the Romans to spare them, and to refuse quarter even to women and children, as they had done at Avaricum; while some were let down from the walls and gave themselves up to the soldiers. Lucius Fabius, a centurion of the 8th legion, who was known to have said that day, in the hearing of his men, that he was fired by the recollection of the rewards that had been offered at Avaricum, and would suffer no man to mount the wall before him, got three men of his company, and, being hoisted up by them, clambered up the wall; then in turn hauling them up one by one, he lifted them on to it.

Meanwhile the men who, as we have pointed out above, had assembled near the other end of the town to fortify the position, heard the outcry, and presently, stimulated by a succession of messages, telling that the town was in the hands of the Romans, sent on horsemen ahead, and hurried up at a great pace. Each man, as he successively arrived, took his stand under the wall and swelled the number of his comrades. And now a great multitude had assembled, and the matrons, who a moment before had been holding out their hands to the Romans from the wall, began to adjure their men-folk and displayed their streaming locks, as Gallic women do, and brought out their children for all to see. It was no fair fight for the Romans. The ground was unfavorable; their numbers were inferior; and, tired out by their rapid climb and the protracted combat, they could not well hold their own against men who had just come fresh into action.

Caesar, seeing that the fight was not on a fair field, and that the enemy's force was increasing became anxious for the safety of his men, and sent an order to Titus Sextius, the general whom he had left in charge of the smaller camp, to take his cohorts out quickly and form them up at the foot of the hill, on the enemy's right flank, so as to check their pursuit in case he saw our men driven from their position. Advancing a little with his own legion from the position which he had taken up, he awaited the issue of the combat.

Fierce fighting was going on, the enemy relying upon position and numbers, our men upon valour, when suddenly the Aedui, whom Caesar had sent up by another path on the right, to create a diversion, were descried on our exposed flank. Being armed like Gauls, they caused a violent panic among our men; and although it was noticed that their right shoulders were bare—the recognized symbol of peace—yet the soldiers fancied that they were foes and had done this on purpose to deceive them. At the same moment the centurion, Lucius Fabius, and the men who had climbed the wall along with him, were surrounded and killed, and their bodies pitched down from the wall. Marcus Petronius, a centurion of the same legion, made an attempt to hew down the gates, but, overwhelmed by numbers, desperate, and covered with wounds, he said to the men of his company who had followed him, "Since I cannot save myself and you, I will, at all events, try to save your lives, for it was I, in my lust for glory, who brought you into danger. You have your chance: use it!" With these words he dashed in among the enemy, killed two of them, and forced the rest back a little way from the gate. His men attempted to help him. "It's useless," he cried, "for you to try to save my life, for blood and strength are ebbing. Go, then, while you have the chance, and return to your legion." So he fought, and soon fell; and so he saved his men.

Overborne at every point, the Romans were driven from their position with the loss of forty-six centurions. The Gauls were relentlessly pursuing when the 10th legion, which had taken post in reserve on comparatively favourable ground, checked them; and the 10th was in its turn supported by the cohorts of the 13th, which had quitted the smaller camp under Titus Sextius, and occupied a commanding position. The moment the legions reached the plain they halted and showed a bold front to the enemy; and Vercingetorix withdrew his men from the foot of the hill into his entrenchments. Nearly seven hundred men were lost that day.

Next day Caesar paraded his troops, and reprimanded them for the rashness and impetuosity which they had shown in judging for themselves how far they were to advance and what they were to do, not halting when the signal was given for recall, and refusing to submit to the control of the tribunes and the generals. He explained that an unfavorable position made a serious difference; he had experienced this himself at Avaricum, when, though he had the enemy in his grasp without their general and without their cavalry, he had an assured triumph for fear the unfavorable ground should entail a loss, however slight, in the action. He heartily admired their heroic spirit, which entrenched camp and high mountain and walled fortress were powerless to daunt; but just as heartily he reprobated their contempt for discipline and their presumption in imagining that they knew how to win battles and forecast results better than their general. He required from his soldiers obedience and self-control just as much as courage and heroism. After this harangue Caesar, in conclusion, encouraged the men, telling them not to let an incident like this trouble them, and not to ascribe losses to the enemy's courage a result which had been brought about by the unfavorable nature of the ground. His intention of abandoning Gergovia being unchanged, he led the legions out of camp, and formed them in line of battle on a good position. Still Vercingetorix did not venture down on to the level. A cavalry skirmish followed, which resulted in favor of the Romans; and Caesar then withdrew his army into camp. Next day he fought a similar action; and then, thinking that he had done enough to humble the vainglory of the Gauls and to restore the confidence of his soldiers, he marched for the country of the Aedui. Even then the enemy did not pursue. Two days later Caesar repaired a bridge over the Allier and threw his army across.

At this Stage the Aeduans, Viridomarus and Eporedorix, approached and accosted him. He learned that Litaviccus had gone off with all the cavalry to work upon the Aedui. It was essential, they urged, that they should be beforehand, in order to keep the tribe steady. By this time Caesar saw clearly from many signs that the Aedui were traitors, and he was of opinion that the departure of these men would hasten their defection: still he did not think it right to detain them; for he desired to avoid the semblance of injustice and not lay himself open to the suspicion of fear. As they were leaving he told them briefly what he had done for the Aedui, pointing out how they were situated and how low they had fallen when his connection with them began, — driven into their strongholds, their lands confiscated, and their allies all taken from them, tribute imposed upon them and hostages wrung from them with the grossest insults; then how he had raised them to such prosperity and power that they not only regained their former position but acquired, in the sight of all, a prestige and influence which they had never enjoyed before. With this reminder he let them go.

There was an Aeduan town, advantageously situated on the banks of the Loire, called Noviodunum. Thither Caesar had conveyed all the hostages of Gaul, his grain, the public monies, and a large portion of his own baggage and that of the army: thither, too, he had sent a large number of horses, which he had purchased in Italy and Spain for the war. On reaching the town, Eporedorix and Viridomarus ascertained the attitude of their tribe: Litaviccus had been received by the Aedui at Bibracte, the most influential town in the country; Convictolitavis, the first magistrate, and a large proportion of the council had assembled to meet him; and envoys had been officially dispatched to Vercingetorix to effect a friendly understanding. An opportunity like this, they thought, was not to be missed. Accordingly they massacred the guard at Noviodunum and the individuals who had settled there for trade, and divided the treasure and the horses; arranged for the conveyance of the hostages of the several tribes to the magistrate at Bibracte; burned the town, which they considered it impossible to hold, to prevent its being of use to the Romans; carried away in barges as much grain as they could hurriedly stow away; and threw the rest into the river or burned it. They then proceeded to raise forces from the neighboring districts, establishing detachments and piquets along the banks of the Loire, and throwing out cavalry in all directions to terrorize the Romans, in the hope of being able to prevent them from getting corn or to drive them, under stress of destitution, to make for the Province. It was a strong point in their favor that the Loire was swollen from the melting of the snow, so that, to all appearance, it was quite unfordable.

On learning this, Caesar decided that he must act at once, in case it should be necessary to take the risk of bridging the river, he might be able to fight before reinforcements came up. To change his whole plan of campaign and march for the Province,—that, he deemed, was a course to which he ought not to allow even the pressure of fear to force him; for the disgrace and the humiliation of retreat, the barrier interposed by the Cevennes, and the condition of the roads forbade him to attempt it; and above all he was intensely anxious for Labienus, who was separated from him, and for the legions which he had placed under his command. Accordingly he made a series of extraordinary marches by day and night; reached the Loire before anyone had expected him; and discovered a ford by the help of the cavalry, which was good enough for an emergency (the men being just able to keep their arms and shoulders above water, to carry their weapons). The cavalry were formed in line to break the force of the current; and, the enemy flying in confusion at the first sight of the army, he brought it safely across. Having satisfied its wants with corn and large numbers of cattle, which he found in the district, he pushed on for the country of the Senones.

While Caesar was engaged in these operations, Labienus marched for Lutetia with his four legions, leaving the draft which had recently arrived from Italy at Agedincum, to protect the heavy baggage. Lutetia is a town belonging to the Parisii, situated on an island in the river Seine. When the enemy became aware of his approach, large forces assembled from the neighboring tribes. The chief command was conferred upon an Aulercan, named Camulogenus, who, though old and worn, was called to this high place because of his uncommon knowledge of war. Observing that there was a continuous marsh, which drained into the Seine and rendered the whole country in its neighborhood impassable, Labienus at first formed a line of sheds and attempted to fill up the marsh with fascines and other material and thus make a causeway to march across. Finding this scarcely practicable, he silently quitted his camp in the third watch, and made his way, by the route by which he had advanced, to Metiosedum, a town belonging to the Senones, situated, like Lutetia, of which we have just spoken, on an island in the Seine. Labienus seized about fifty barges, rapidly lashed them together, and threw the troops on to them: the townspeople, many of whom had been summoned into the field, were paralyzed with astonishment and fear; and Labienus took the town without a blow. After repairing the bridge, which the enemy had recently broken down, he made the army cross over, and marched on, following the course of the stream, in the direction of Lutetia. The enemy, informed of what he had done by fugitives from Metiosedum, gave orders that Lutetia should be burned and its bridges broken down: then, moving away from the marsh, they encamped on the banks of the Seine, opposite Lutetia and over against the camp of Labienus.

By this time it was known that Caesar had abandoned his position at Gergovia: by this. time too rumors were arriving about the defection of the Aedui and the success of the Gallic insurrection; and the Gauls affirmed that Caesar was prevented from pursuing his march and from crossing the Loire, and that want of corn had forced him to make a dash for the Province. The Bellovaci, moreover, who were already and spontaneously disaffected, on learning that the Aedui had gone over, began to raise troops and to make overt preparations for war. Now that the situation had so completely changed, Labienus saw that he must completely alter his original plan: what he thought of now was not how to gain some positive advantage and force the enemy to an engagement, but how to get his army safely back to Agedincum. On one side he was menaced by the Bellovaci, who have the greatest reputation for fighting as any tribe in Gaul; on the other Camulogenus held the field with a well-found army, ready for action; while a great river separated the legions from their baggage and the troops which protected it. With these formidable difficulties suddenly confronting him, he saw that he must look for aid to the force of his own character.

Towards evening he assembled his officers, and, charging them to carry out his orders to the letter, placed one of the Roman knights in charge of each of the barges which he had brought down from Metiosedum, and ordered them to move silently four miles downstream at the end of the first watch, and wait for him there. Leaving five cohorts, which he believed to be the least steady in action, to hold the camp, he ordered the remaining five of the same legion to move up the river about midnight with the whole baggage-train, and make a great noise. He also procured a number of small boats, and sent them in the same direction, the rowers making a great splash with their oars. Soon afterwards he silently moved out of camp with three legions, and made for the spot to which he had ordered the barges to be rowed.

When the legions reached the spot, the enemy's patrols were surprised at their posts all along the river by our troops—for a great storm had sprung up suddenly—and cut down. Infantry and cavalry were swiftly ferried across under the superintendence of the Roman knights, whom Labienus had charged with the duty. Just before dawn and almost simultaneously the enemy were informed that an unusual commotion was going on in the Roman camp; that a large column was moving up the river, and the sound of oars audible in the same direction; and that troops were being ferried across a little lower down. On hearing this, they imagined that the legions were crossing at three places, and that the Romans, in alarm at the defection of the Aedui, were all preparing for flight. Accordingly they made a corresponding distribution of their own troops. Leaving a force opposite the Roman camp, and sending a small body in the direction of Metiosedum, with orders to advance as far as the boats had gone, they led the rest of their troops against Labienus.

By daybreak the whole of our troops were ferried across and the enemy's line was discernible. Labienus, bidding the soldiers remember their ancient valour and their many splendid victories, and imagine that Caesar, under whose command they had many times beaten the enemy, was present in person, gave the signal for action. At the first onset, the right wing, where the 7th legion stood, drove back the enemy and put them to flight. The 12th legion occupied the left. There the enemy's foremost ranks fell, transfixed by javelins: but the other ranks vigorously resisted; and not a man laid himself open to the suspicion of cowardice. Camulogenus, the enemy's commander, supported his men by his presence and cheered them on. And now, when victory was still doubtful, the tribunes of the 7th legion, who had been told of what was passing on the left wing, made the legion show itself on the enemy's rear, and charged. Even in that moment not a man quitted his post; but all were surrounded and slain. Camulogenus shared their fate. The detachment which had been left on guard opposite Labienus's camp, on hearing that the battle had begun, went to the support of their comrades and occupied a hill; but they could not withstand the onset of our victorious soldiery. Mingling with their flying comrades, they were slain—all who failed to find shelter in the woods and on the hills—by the Roman cavalry. Labienus's task was accomplished. He returned to Agedincum, where he had left the heavy baggage of the whole army, and thence made his way, with his entire force, to the quarters of Caesar.

When the defection of the Aedui became known the gravity of the war increased. Embassies were dispatched in all directions, the Aedui exerting all their influence, prestige, and pecuniary resources to win over the tribes; and, having in their power the hostages whom Caesar had left in their country, they intimidated waverers by threatening to kill them. They requested Vercingetorix to visit them and concert with them a plan of campaign; and when he complied, they insisted that the supreme control should be transferred to them. The demand was disputed; and a Pan-Gallic council was convened at Bibracte. Delegates flocked thither in numbers. The question was put to the vote; and the delegates unanimously confirmed the appointment of Vercingetorix as commander-in-chief. The Remi, Lingones, and Treveri were not represented in the council,—the two former because they adhered to their friendship with the Romans; the Treveri because they were far away and were themselves hard pressed by the Germans, for which reason they kept aloof all through the war and remained neutral. The Aedui, bitterly chagrined at being ousted from the supremacy, lamented their change of fortune and sorely missed Caesar's favor; yet, having taken up arms, they dared not sever themselves from the other tribes. Reluctantly those ambitious young leaders, Eporedorix and Viridomarus, obeyed Vercingetorix.

The commander-in-chief ordered the newly joined tribes to give hostages, fixing a date for their arrival, and directed all the cavalry, numbering fifteen thousand, to assemble speedily. He announced that he would content himself with the infantry which he had already, and would not tempt fortune by fighting a battle, for, as he was strong in cavalry, it would be quite easy to prevent the Romans from getting corn and forage: only let the patriots destroy their own corn and burn their homesteads in the certainty that by this personal sacrifice they were securing independence and liberty for evermore, Having made these arrangements, he ordered the Aedui and the Segusiavi, who are conterminous with the Province, to furnish ten thousand infantry, which he reinforced by eight hundred cavalry, and, placing Eporedorix's brother in command, directed him to attack the Allobroges. In another quarter, he sent the Gabali and the Arvernian clans nearest to the Helvii to attack that people, and the Ruteni and Cadurci to devastate the territory of the Volcae Arecomici. At the same time he attempted by secret emissaries and embassies to gain over the Allobroges, promising money to the leading men, and to the tribe dominion over the whole Province; for he hoped that they had not yet forgotten the late war.

To meet these emergencies there were detachments in readiness, amounting to twenty-two cohorts, which had been raised by Lucius from the whole Province, and were posted to meet every attack. The Helvii, who encountered the neighboring clans on their own, were defeated with the loss of Gaius Valerius Domnotaurus, the first magistrate, and many others, and forced to take refuge in strongholds and behind walls. The Allobroges posted a chain of piquets along the Rhone, and defended their own territory with great care and vigilance. Caesar, being aware of the enemy's superiority in cavalry, and unable to get any assistance from the Province and Italy as all the roads were blocked, sent across the Rhine to the tribes of Germany which he had subdued in former years, and called into the field cavalry with the light-armed foot which habitually fight in their rank's. On their arrival, as their horses were unserviceable, he took those of the tribunes and other Roman knights and also of the time-expired volunteers, and assigned them to the Germans.

During these operations the enemy's forces and the cavalry levied from Vercingetorix were assembling to attack him. Vercingetorix collected a large number of these troops, and while Caesar was marching through the most distant part of the country of the Lingones which was furthest from his [Caesar's] starting-point in the direction in which he was going, that is, towards the country of the Sequani, that he might be in a better position for reinforcing the Province, took post in three camps about ten miles from the Romans. Summoning his cavalry officers to a council of war, he told them that the hour of victory had come: the Romans were retreating to the Province and abandoning Gaul. This would secure liberty for the time: but for lasting peace and tranquility the gain was small; for they would come back in increased force and continue the war indefinitely. The cavalry, then, must attack them on the march, while they were helpless. If the infantry stopped to support their comrades, they could not continue their march: if, as he thought more likely, they abandoned their baggage and tried to save themselves, they would lose indispensable materiel as well as prestige. As for the enemy's cavalry, they at any rate ought not to doubt that not a man of them would dare so much as stir outside the column. To encourage them in their attack, he would post all his troops in front of the camps and overawe the enemy. With one voice the knights exclaimed that every man must be sworn by a solemn oath to ride twice through the enemy's column, or never be admitted beneath a roof, never come nigh unto children, or parents, or wife.

The proposal was approved; and every man was sworn. Next day the cavalry were divided into three sections, two of which made a demonstration on either flank, while the third checked the advance of the vanguard. When the movement was reported, Caesar in turn divided his cavalry into three parts, and ordered them to advance against the enemy. The combat became general. The column halted; and the baggage was brought into the intervals between the legions. When, at any point, our men appeared to be in difficulties or actually overmatched, Caesar made the infantry advance in their direction and form in line. These tactics prevented the enemy from following up their advantage, and encouraged our men by the assurance of support. At length the Germans occupied the summit of a ridge on the right flank, dislodged the enemy, and drove them in rout with heavy loss to a stream where Vercingetorix had taken post with his infantry. Observing this, the rest of the cavalry were afraid of being surrounded, and took to flight. The whole field was a scene of carnage. Three Aeduans of the highest rank were brought prisoners to Caesar,—Cotus, commandant of the cavalry, who had disputed the claims of Convictolitavis at the recent election; Cavarillus, who had taken command of the infantry after the defection of Litaviccus; and Eporedorix, who had commanded the Aedui in their war with the Sequani before Caesar's arrival.

After the total defeat of his cavalry, Vercingetorix withdrew his infantry from the position which he had taken up in front of the fortress camps, and, ordering his baggage-train to leave camp quickly and follow him, marched forthwith for Alesia, a stronghold of the Mandubii. Caesar removed his baggage to a hill close by, and, leaving two legions to guard it, kept up the pursuit as long as daylight permitted, killing about three thousand of the enemy's rearguard, and encamped next day in the neighborhood of Alesia. The enemy were cowed by the defeat of their cavalry, the arm in which they had the greatest confidence; accordingly, after reconnoitering the position, he called upon the soldiers to brace themselves for an effort and proceeded to form a contravallation.

The fortress stood on the top of a hill, in a very commanding position, being apparently impregnable except by blockade. The base of the hill was washed on two sides by two streams. In front of the town extended a plain about three miles in length; and on every other side it was surrounded, at a moderate distance, by hills of elevation equal to its own. Below the wall, on the side of the hill which looked towards the east, the whole space was crowded with the Gallic troops, who had fortified it with a ditch and a wall of loose stones, six feet high. The perimeter of the works which the Romans were about to construct covered eleven miles. Camps were established in convenient positions; and in their neighborhood twenty-three redoubts were constructed, in which piquets were posted during the day, to prevent any sudden sortie, while at night they were guarded by strong bivouacs. After the commencement of the works a cavalry combat took place in the plain which, as we have explained above, formed a gap in the hills, extending three miles in length. Both sides fought their hardest. As our men were in difficulties, Caesar sent the Germans to support them, and drew up the legions in front of the camps to prevent any sudden attack by the enemy's infantry. Supported by the legions, our men gathered confidence: the enemy were put to flight, and, hampered by their own numbers, got jammed in the gateways, which had been left too narrow. The Germans hotly pursued them right up to the entrenchments. The carnage was great, and some of the fugitives dismounted and tried to cross the ditch and climb over the wall. Caesar ordered the legions which he had drawn up in front of the ramparts to advance a little. The Gauls inside the entrenchments were not less terrified than the fugitives, and, believing that they would speedily be attacked, shouted "To arms"; while some rushed panic-stricken into the town. Vercingetorix ordered the gates to be shut, to prevent the camp from being deserted; and the Germans, having killed a great many men and captured a number of horses, returned.

Vercingetorix now determined to send away all his cavalry in the night before the Romans had time to complete the entrenchments. As they were moving off, he bade them go, every man to his own country, and make all who were of an age to bear arms take the field. Reminding them of his own services, he adjured them to have some regard for his safety and not . to give up one who had served so well the cause of national liberty to be tortured by the enemy. If they did not bestir themselves, he told them, eighty thousand picked men would perish with him. He calculated that he had corn enough to last barely thirty days: but by reducing the rations it might be possible to hold out a little. longer. With these instructions he silently sent out the cavalry through a gap in the works. He ordered all the grain to be brought to him, giving notice that those who disobeyed should be put to death; distributed the livestock, of which a great quantity had been driven in by the Mandubii, individually among the garrison; made arrangements for doling out the grain gradually; and withdrew into the town all the forces which he had posted in front of it. In this way he prepared to fight on and await the Gallic reinforcements.

Being informed of what had passed by deserters and prisoners, Caesar planned defensive works of the following kind. Constructing a trench twenty feet wide with vertical sides, the width at the bottom being exactly equal to the distance between its upper edges, he traced out all the remaining works eight hundred paces behind it, his object being, as he was obliged to cover such a vast extent of ground and it was not easy to man the whole system of works with an unbroken ring of troops, to prevent the enemy from swooping down unexpectedly upon the lines in force at night, or in the day-time discharging missiles at the men while they were at work. Leaving this interval, he dug two trenches of equal depth, each fifteen feet wide, and filled the inner one, where it crossed the plain and the low ground, with water drawn from the stream. Behind the trenches he constructed a rampart and palisade twelve feet high, which he strengthened by an embattled breastwork, with large forked branches projecting along the line where the breastwork joined the rampart, to check the ascent of the enemy; and erected towers on the entire circuit of the works at intervals of eighty feet.

While these vast fortifications were being constructed, it was necessary to fetch timber and corn; and the troops, having to move considerable distances from camp, were unavoidably weakened. Sometimes, indeed, the Gauls attempted to storm our works and made furious sallies from the town by several gates. Caesar therefore thought it necessary to strengthen the works still further, in order to render the lines defensible by a smaller force. Accordingly trees or very stout branches were cut down and their ends stripped of their bark and sharpened to a point; continuous trenches were then dug, five feet deep, in which the logs were planted and fastened down at the bottom to prevent their being dragged out, while the boughs projected above. There were five rows in each trench, connected with one another and interlaced; and all who stepped in would impale themselves on the sharp stakes. The men called them "grave-stones." In front of them, arranged in slanting rows in the form of a quincunx, pits were dug, three feet deep, which tapered gradually towards the bottom. Smooth logs, as thick as a man's thigh, sharpened at the top and hardened by fire, were planted in them, projecting not more than four fingers above the ground. At the same time the earth was trampled down to the depth of one foot above the bottom, to keep them firmly in position; while the rest of the pit was covered with twigs and brushwood to hide the trap. There were eight rows of this kind, three feet apart. The men called them lilies, from their resemblance to that flower. In front of them blocks of wood a foot long, with barbed iron spikes let into them, were completely buried in the earth and scattered about in all directions at moderate intervals. The men called them "spurs."

When these defenses were completed, Caesar constructed, along the most suitable tracts which the lie of the country enabled him to follow, embracing a circuit of fourteen miles, corresponding works of the same kind, facing the opposite way, to repel the enemy from without, so as to prevent the troops who defended the lines from being hemmed in by any force, however numerous; and, in order to avoid the danger of having to leave camp, he directed all the troops to provide themselves with fodder and corn for thirty days.

While this was going on at Alesia, the Gauls convened a council of their leading men, who decided not to adopt Vercingetorix's plan of assembling all who could bear arms, but to levy a definite contingent from each tribe; for they were afraid that with such a vast multitude crowding together they would not be able to control their respective contingents or keep them apart, or to organize any system for providing grain. The Aedui with their dependents, the Segusiavi, Ambivareti, and Aulerci Bran-novices, were ordered to find thirty-five thousand men; the Arverni, along with the Eleuteti, Cadurci, Gabali, and Vellavii, who are habituated to their sway, the same number; the Sequani, Senones, Bituriges, Santoni, Ruteni, and Carnutes, each twelve thousand; the Bellovaci, ten thousand, and the Lemovices the same; the Pictones, Turoni, Parisii, and Helvetii, each eight thousand; the Andes, Ambiani, Mediomatrici, Petrocorii, Nervii, Morini, and Nitiobroges, each six thousand; the Aulerci Cenomani, five thousand, and the Atrebates the same; the Vellocasses, four thousand; the Aulerci Eburovices three thousand; the Rauraci and Boii, each two thousand; and all the maritime tribes conjointly, which the Gauls usually call Armorican, including the Coriosolites, Redones, Ambibarii, Caletes, Osismi, Veneti, Lemovices, and Venelli, thirty thousand. The Bellovaci did not furnish their proper contingent, saying that they would fight the Romans on their own account, just as they pleased, and not submit to the dictation of any one; however, at the request of Commius, and in consideration of their friendly relations with him, they sent two thousand men along with the rest.

Caesar, as we have already mentioned, had found Commius a loyal and serviceable agent in former years in Britain; and, in acknowledgment of these services, he had granted his tribe immunity from taxation, restored to it its rights and laws, and placed the Morini under his authority. Yet so intense was the unanimous determination of the entire Gallic people to establish their liberty and recover their ancient military renown that no favors, no recollection of former friendship, had any influence with them, but all devoted their energies and resources to the prosecution of the war. Eight thousand horse and about two hundred and fifty thousand foot were raised. They were reviewed and numbered in the country of the Aedui, and their officers appointed. The Atrebatian, Commius, the two Aeduans, Viridomarus and Eporedorix, and Vercassivellaunus, an Arvernian and kinsman of Vercingetorix, were entrusted with the command. Delegates from the various tribes were associated with them, in accordance with whose advice they were to conduct the campaign. All started for Alesia in high spirits and full of confidence; and there was not one of them who did not believe that the mere appearance of so vast a host would be irresistible especially as the fighting would be on two fronts, the besieged sallying forth from the town, while without would be conspicuous those huge hosts of cavalry and infantry.

But the besieged in Alesia knew nothing of what was going on in the country of the Aedui; cannibalism, which they had expected their countrymen to succor them was past; and their grain was all consumed. A council of war was therefore convened; and they considered what was to become of them. Various opinions were mooted. Some advised surrender; others a sortie while their strength held out; but Critognatus, an Arvernian of noble family and acknowledged influence, made a speech, which, in view of its singular and atrocious cruelty, ought not, I think, to be passed over. "I do not intend," he said, "to notice the view of those who dignify the most abject slavery by the title of surrender; for I hold that they ought not to be counted as citizens or admitted to a council. I am only concerned with those who are in favor of a sortie; for, as you are all agreed, in their counsel is to be recognized the memory of our ancient valour. To be unable to bear privation for a short span,—that I call weakness, not manly resolution. It is easier to find men who will affront death than men who will patiently endure suffering. And yet I would give my sanction to this view—so highly do I respect the authority of its advocates—if I saw no evil involved in it save the sacrifice of our own lives; but in forming our plans we must have regard to the whole of Gaul, for we have called upon the whole of Gaul to help us. If eighty thousand men fall on one field, what, think you, will be the feelings of our friends and kinsmen, when they are constrained to fight almost on the very corpses of the slain? To save you, they have counted their personal danger as nothing; do not, then, rob them of your aid; do not, by your folly and rashness or lack of resolution, ruin the whole of Gaul and subject it to perpetual slavery. Can it be that, because they have not arrived punctually to the day, you doubt their good faith and resolution? What then? Do you suppose that the Romans are toiling day after day on those outer lines, simply to amuse themselves? If the messengers of your countrymen cannot reassure you because all ingress is barred, accept Roman testimony that their coming is near: dread of that event keeps them busy upon their works night and day. What, then, is my counsel I counsel you to do what our fathers did in their war with the Cimbri and Teutoni,—a war in no way comparable to this: forced into their strongholds and brought low, like us, by famine, they kept themselves alive by feeding upon the flesh of those whose age disqualified them for war; but they did not surrender to the enemy. And if we had no precedent for this, still, in the name of liberty, I would hold it a most glorious precedent to create and bequeath to posterity. For what resemblance was there between that war and this? The Cimbri devastated Gaul and brought upon her grievous calamity; but they did at last leave our country and seek other lands; they did leave us our rights, our laws, our lands, our liberty. But the Romans, what aim, what purpose have they but this,—from mere envy to settle in the lands and tribal territories of a people whose renown and warlike prowess they have come to know, and to fasten upon them the yoke of everlasting slavery? Never have they made war on any other principle. If you know not what is going on among distant peoples, look at the Gaul on your border: reduced to a province, its rights and laws revolutionized, prostrate beneath the lictor's axe, it is crushed by perpetual slavery."

The votes were recorded. It was decided that those whose age or infirmity disqualified them for fighting should leave the town; that the rest should try every expedient before having recourse to Critognatus's proposal; but that, if circumstances were too strong and the reinforcements delayed, they should adopt it rather than stoop to accept terms of surrender or peace. The Mandubii, who had admitted them into the town, were compelled to leave with their wives and children. When they reached the lines, they earnestly entreated the Romans with tears to receive them as slaves,—only give them something to eat. But Caesar posted guards on the rampart, and forbade them admission from our entrenchments. Next day they moved their cavalry out of camp, occupied the whole plain which, as we have shown, extends three miles in length, and, drawing back their infantry a little, posted them on the high ground. The town of Alesia commanded a view over the plain. Descrying the reinforcements, the besieged crowded together and congratulated each other; and all were joyfully excited. Leading their forces to the front, they took post before the town, filled up the nearest trench with fascines covered with earth, and made ready for a sortie and for every hazard.

Disposing his whole force on both lines of entrenchment, so that every man might know his cavalry. proper place and keep it, ready for emergencies, Caesar ordered the cavalry to move out of camp and engage. All the camps which crowned the surrounding heights commanded a view of the field; and all the soldiers were intently awaiting the issue of the combat. Here and there among their cavalry the Gauls had scattered archers and active light-armed foot, to support their comrades in case they gave way, and withstand the charges of our cavalry. A good many men were wounded by these troops, whose attack they had not foreseen, and left the field. Feeling sure that their countrymen were winning, and observing that our men were being overpowered by numbers, the beleaguered Gauls, as well as those who had come to rescue them, cheered and yelled on every side to encourage their comrades. As the fighting was going on in full view of every one, and no gallant deed, no cowardice, could escape notice, love of glory and fear of disgrace stimulated both sides to valour. From noon till near sunset the fight went on; and still the issue was doubtful. At length the Germans massed their squadrons at one point, and charged and forced back the enemy; and on their flight the archers were surrounded and slain. The other divisions likewise falling back, our men gave them no chance of rallying, but pursued them right up to their encampment. The besieged, who had sallied forth from Alesia, well-nigh despairing of success, sadly retreated into the town.

An interval of one day followed, during which the Gauls made a great quantity of fascines, ladders, and grappling-hooks fixed to long poles. At midnight they moved silently out of camp and advanced to the entrenchments in the plain. Suddenly they raised a shout to inform the besieged of their approach, and began to throw their fascines, to drive the Romans from the rampart with slings, arrows, and stones, and in every other way to press the attack. Simultaneously Vercingetorix, hearing the distant cry, sounded the trumpet and led his men out of the town. Our troops moved up to the entrenchments, in the places which had been severally allotted to them beforehand, and drove back the Gauls with slings throwing large stones and sharp stakes which they had laid at intervals on the rampart, and with bullets. The darkness made it impossible to see clearly, and on both sides many were wounded; while missiles were hurled in showers by the artillery. Two generals, Mark Antony and Gains Trebonius, who had been charged with the defense of this part of the lines, withdrew troops from the distant redoubts, and reinforced our men at every point where they saw them overmatched.

So long as the Gauls kept at a distance from the entrenchment, the number of their missiles gave them the advantage; but when they came closer, some trod unawares upon the "spurs," others tumbled into the pits and impaled themselves, while others were transfixed by heavy pikes from the rampart and towers, and perished. Everywhere they suffered heavy loss, and at no point did they break the lines. Towards daybreak, fearing that they might be attacked from the higher camps on their exposed flank and surrounded, they fell back and rejoined their comrades. The besieged lost much time in bringing out the implements which Vercingetorix had prepared for the sortie, and in filling up the nearer trench; and finding, before they could approach the contravallation, that their comrades had withdrawn, they went back unsuccessful to the town.

Having been twice repulsed with heavy loss, the Gauls considered what was to be done. They called in natives who were familiar with the ground, and ascertained from them the position of the higher camps and the nature of their fortifications. There was a hill on the north which had such a wide sweep that the Romans had not been able to include it within the circumvallation, and were obliged to make the camp there on a gentle slope, which gave an assailant a slight advantage. This camp was garrisoned by two legions under the command of two generals, Gaius Antistius Reginus and

Gaius Caninius Rebilus. After making a reconnaissance, the hostile leaders selected from the whole force sixty thousand men belonging to the tribes which had the highest reputation for valour, secretly decided on their plan of operations, and fixed the attack for noon. Vercassivellaunus, an Arvernian, one of the four generals and a relation of Vercingetorix, was placed in command of the force. He left camp in the first watch: towards daybreak he had almost finished his march; and, concealing himself behind the hill, he ordered his soldiers to rest after the toil of the night. Towards noon he pushed on for the camp mentioned above; and simultaneously the cavalry began to move towards the entrenchments in the plain, while the rest of the host made a demonstration in front of their camp.

Descrying his countrymen from the citadel of Alesia, Vercingetorix moved out of the town, taking from the camp the long pikes, sappers, grappling-hooks, and other implements which he had prepared for the sortie. Fighting went on simultaneously at every point; and the besieged tried every expedient, concentrating their strength on the weakest points. The Roman forces, being strung out over lines of vast extent, found it hard to move to several points at once. The shouts of the combatants in their rear had a serious effect in unnerving the men, who saw that their own lives were staked upon the courage of others; for men are generally disquieted most by the unseen.

Caesar found a good position, from which he observed all the phases of the action and reinforced those who were in difficulties. Both sides saw that now was the moment for a supreme effort: the Gauls utterly despaired of safety unless they could break the lines; the Romans, if they could but hold their ground, looked forward to the end of all their toils. The struggle was most severe at the entrenchments on the high ground, against which, as we have remarked, Vercassivellaunus had been sent. The unfavorable downward slope told heavily. Some of the assailants showered in missiles, while others locked their shields above their heads, and advanced to the assault; and when they were tired, fresh men took their places. The entire force shot earth against the fortifications, which at once enabled the Gauls to ascend and buried the obstacles which the Romans had hidden in the ground. And now weapons, and strength to use them were failing our men.

On learning the state of affairs, Caesar sent Labienus with six cohorts to rescue the hard-pressed garrison, telling him, in case he could not hold on, to lead out the cohorts and charge, but only as a forlorn hope. Visiting the other divisions in person, he adjured them not to give in: on that day, he told them, on that hour was staked the prize of all past combats. The besieged, abandoning the hope of forcing the formidable works in the plain, took the implements which they had prepared and attempted to storm a steep ascent. With a hail of missiles they drove off the men who defended the towers, filled up the trenches with earth and fascines, and with their grappling-hooks tore down the rampart and breastworks.

Caesar first sent the younger Brutus with a number of cohorts, and afterwards Gaius Fabius with others: finally, as the fighting grew fiercer, he led a fresh detachment in person to the rescue. Having restored the battle and beaten off the enemy, he hastened to the point to which he had dispatched Labienus, withdrawing four cohorts from the nearest redoubt, and ordering part of the cavalry to follow him and part to ride round the outer lines and attack the enemy in the rear. Labienus, finding that neither rampart nor trench could check the enemy's onslaught, massed eleven cohorts, which he was fortunately able to withdraw from the nearest piquets, and sent messengers to let Caesar know what he intended. Caesar hastened to take part in the action.

The enemy knew that he was coming from the color of his cloak, which he generally wore in action to mark his identity, and, catching sight of the cohorts and troops of cavalry which he had ordered to follow him, descending the incline, which was plainly discernible from their commanding position, began the attack. Both sides raised a cheer, and the cheering was taken up along the rampart and the whole extent of the lines. Our men dropped their javelins and plied their swords. Suddenly the cavalry was seen on the enemy's rear: the fresh cohorts came up; the enemy turned tail; and the cavalry charged the fugitives. The carnage was great. Sedulius, commander and chieftain of the Lemovices, was slain; Vercassivellaunus, the Arvernian, was taken alive as he was trying to escape: seventy-four standards were brought to Caesar; and few of that mighty host got safely back to camp. Descrying from the town the slaughter and the rout of their countrymen, the besieged in despair recalled their troops from the entrenchments. Hearing this, the Gauls in camp forthwith fled; and if the soldiers had not been tired out by frequent supporting movements and by the whole day's toil, the enemy's entire host might have been annihilated. The cavalry were dispatched about midnight, and hung upon the rearguard. A large number were captured and slain; the rest escaped and went off to their respective tribes.

Next day Vercingetorix called a council. He explained that he had undertaken the war, not for private ends, but in the cause of national freedom; and, since they must needs bow to fortune, he would submit to whichever alternative they preferred,—either to appease the Romans by putting him to death or to surrender him alive. Envoys were sent to refer the question to Caesar. He ordered the arms to be surrendered and the leaders brought out. The officers were conducted to the entrenchment in front of his camp, where he was seated. Vercingetorix surrendered, and the arms were grounded. Caesar allotted one prisoner by way of prize to every man in the army, making an exception in favor of the Aedui and Arverni, as he hoped by restoring them to win back the two tribes.

These arrangements completed, he started for the country of the Aedui, and received the sent envoys, promising to obey his orders; and he ordered them to furnish a large number of hostages. The legions were sent into winter quarters, and about twenty thousand prisoners restored to the Aedui and Arverni. He directed Titus Labienus to march with two legions and. a detachment of cavalry into the country of the Sequani, placing Marcus Sempronius Rutilus under his command; stationed Gaius Fabius and Lucius Minucius Basilus with two legions in the country of the Remi, to protect them from injury at the hands of their neighbors, the Bellovaci; dispatched Gaius Antistius Reginus into the country of the Ambivareti, Titus Sextius into that of the Bituriges, and Gaius Caninius Rebilus into that of the Ruteni,—each in command of a legion; and quartered Quintus Tullius Cicero and Publius Sulpicius in the country of the Aedui at Cabillo and Matisco on the Saone, to collect grain.

He decided to winter himself at Bibracte. When the results of the campaign were made known by his dispatches, a thanksgiving service of twenty days was held at Rome.

Image Gallery

Roman soldiers in Gaul (Légionnaire romain)

Légionnaire romain (légion gauloise); Bucinator (trompette); Aquila (porte ai...)

Soldiers of Gaul

As imagined by a late 19th C. illustrator for the Larousse dictionary, 1898.

Vercingetorix Throws Down His Arms at the Feet of Julius Caesar

Lionel Noel Royer, 1899.

Cleopatra and Caesar

Jean-Léon Gérôme, 1865.

Abel de Pujol, 1808.

La Mort de César

Jean-Léon Gérôme, 1867.

Jean-Léon Gérôme, 1872.

The Christian Martyrs' Last Prayer

Jean-Léon Gérôme, 1863.

The Death of Caesar

Vincenzo Camuccini, 1798.

Made in the USA
Middletown, DE
24 October 2020

22705622R00094